Irish
Confederates
The Civil War's
Forgotten Soldiers

Irish Confederates
The Civil War's Forgotten Soldiers

Phillip Thomas Tucker

McWhiney Foundation Press
McMurry University
Abilene, Texas

Library of Congress Cataloging-in-Publication Data

Tucker, Phillip Thomas, 1953-
    Irish confederates : the Civil War's forgotten soldiers /
    Phillip Thomas Tucker.
    p. cm.
    Includes bibliographical references and index.
    ISBN-13: 978-1-893114-53-1 (pbk.: alk. paper)
    ISBN-10: 1-893114-53-8 (pbk.: alk. paper)

    1. United States–History–Civil War, 1861-1865–Participation, Irish
American. 2. Irish American soldiers–Confederate States of
America–History. 3. Confederate States of America. Army–History.
4. United States–History–Civil War, 1861-1865–Regimental histories.
5. United States–History–Civil War, 1861-1865–Campaigns. 6. Irish
Americans–Southern States–History–19th century. I. Title.

E585.I75T83 2006
973.7'420899162--dc22

                  2006016120

McWhiney Foundation Press
McMurry Station, Box 637
Abilene, TX 79697-0637
(325) 572-3974
(325) 572-3991 fax
www.mcwhiney.org

Printed in the United States of America

Distributed by Texas A&M University Press Consortium
www.tamu.edu/upress
1-800-826-8911

ISBN-10: 1-893114-53-8
ISBN-13: 978-1-893114-53-1
10 9 8 7 6 5 4 3 2 1

Book Designed by Rosenbohm Graphic Design

To a mother of Scotch-Irish decent and blessed with
Irish ways and an Irish sense of humor.

TABLE OF CONTENTS

Photographs and Illustrations

The photographs on pages 15 (bottom), 25, 28, and 55 are from the United States Military History Institute Photo Archives in Carlisle, Pennsylvania. The photograph on page 15 (top) is from *Photographic History of the Civil War*. The photographs from pages 16, 17, 18, 19, 20, 41, 48, 49, 58, 60, 78, 82, 88, and 104 are from the Library of Congress. The illustrations on pages 45, 98, and 105 are from *Harper's Weekly*, and the picture on page 96 is from Texas History Stories, copyright State House Press.

INTRODUCTION

Perhaps no role of any participants in the Civil War has been more misunderstood than that of the Irish. The general assumption has been that Irish Americans fought almost exclusively for the Union, struggling and dying for their adopted country. What is not generally known is that many Irishmen fought and died while in service to the Confederate States of America.

In the words of one Irish Confederate from Missouri: "Whoever tells the truth as to our war will [draw the analogy of] Ireland in her struggle for self-government for Irish blood asserted itself in our war." This conclusion was not an exaggeration. The widespread participation of the Confederate Irish, consisting of the Ireland-born and the sons of immigrants, was in fact extensive. This study focuses upon representative examples of Irish Rebel efforts and sacrifices in the Confederacy's bid for independence. While constituting only a relatively small percentage in the overall Confederate forces, the Confederate Irish were important and should not be forgotten.

The notable absence of the Confederate Irish from the historical record in part reflects the fact that the majority, especially the immigrant Irish, were illiterate. The immigrant

Irish in gray left relatively little behind in regard to primary source material (letters, diaries, memoirs, and journals), even less in fact than what was left by African American soldiers who fought and died for the Union.

Both during the war years and to the present day, popular interest in the most famous ethnic unit of the Civil War, the Irish Brigade of the Army of the Potomac, has also helped to obscure the role of the Confederate Irish. Large numbers of Irish, many of whom had immigrated to the North during the 1840s, served in the Union armies during the Civil War, an estimated 150,000 altogether. Some Southerners, especially the Confederate Irish, believed that this Celtic contribution was decisive in winning victory for the Union. Patrick Condon, an Irish Southerner, said after the war, "Southern people, Irish included [felt] much bitterness against the Irish of the North on account of [their] being regarded . . . as the chief cause of the destruction of the Confederacy."

Irish Confederates were in general longer-term residents of America than the Irish in the North. These Southerners of Irish descent, consequently, possessed a larger stake in the American dream, in part because they had encountered less anti-Irish and anti-Catholic prejudice and more opportunity in the agricultural South than had the Irish in the large northeastern cities, such as New York, Philadelphia, and Boston. In overall terms, the Irish of the South more successfully assimilated into mainstream southern life and society, whereas the Irish of the North, especially the recent immigrants, met with greater prejudice and hostility.

Anti-Irish feelings reached a zenith in America during the 1850s. The best organized and politically-affluent anti-Irish and anti-Catholic power structure in antebellum America was the Know-Nothing Party of the 1850s. This vibrant nativist sentiment among Americans, especially in the North, was a hostile reaction to the hundreds of thousands of impoverished immigrant Irish who poured into the United States during the 1840s and 1850s. This exodus from the Emerald Isle resulted largely from the horrors of the Potato Famine, which destroyed the primary food source of the Irish people, causing widespread starvation and death across the countryside. Both Northerners and Southerners feared that their civilization, culture, and religion were threatened by the influx of Irish with their different culture, religious beliefs, and Celtic-Gaelic traditions. Southern leaders, such as Patrick Ronayne Cleburne and Thomas C. Hindman of Arkansas— both future Confederate generals—strongly opposed the Know-Nothings. Like many other far-sighted Southerners, they realized that the assistance of Irishmen "might soon be required to maintain the South's honor and integrity."

In fact, the South took advantage of the abundance of inexpensive Irish labor, and many, some of them future soldiers, helped improve the South's infrastructure throughout the antebellum period. Irish laborers led the way for the development of the South by building railroads, canals, and roads. Recent Irish Catholic immigrants often supplied the labor, both skilled and unskilled, to accomplish these tedious tasks. In a series of revealing articles written for the *New York Times* during the 1850s, Frederick Law Olmstead recognized the importance of Irish labor in regard to the agricultural production of the antebellum Upper South. Olmstead wrote how Virginia farmers preferred free labor over slave labor, after having employed black and white Virginians, Germans, and then Irish, whom he "had found . . . on the whole the best." In overall terms, the struggle of the Confederate Irish was more to preserve their gains already won in southern society rather than attempting to demonstrate their worth as American citizens. Soldiers of the Union Irish Brigade, on the other hand, more often risked their lives on the battlefield to disprove long-existing negative stereotypes in a bid to open up the doors to greater opportunity and acceptance for the Irish across the North.

Southern life and society were far more influenced by the section's rich and vibrant Celtic roots than the North. While northern society in 1861 was primarily a transplanted English culture, the South was in essence an extended Celtic nation, consisting mostly of descendants and immigrants primarily from Ireland, Scotland, and Wales. Throughout the Eighteenth Century, the Scotch-Irish from northern Ireland, mainly from the province of Ulster, settled along the sprawling southern frontier, stretching south for hundreds of miles from western Pennsylvania to South Carolina. Dr. Grady McWhiney was the first American historian to articulate fully the overall importance of the Irish experience in the South's settlement and the extensive Celtic contribution to southern culture and society. This distinctive Celtic contribution in America's development continued with later day immigrants, especially the Potato Famine Irish, who arrived during the 1840s. In general, the South gained large numbers of Scotch-Irish Protestants starting in the colonial period before the American Revolution, and large numbers of Irish Catholics from the Potato Famine of the 1840s. The dominance of slavery in the South ensured that the Irish, recent immigrants or long-time residents, would not occupy the lowest rung of society.

The estimated 30,000 Confederate Irish who served in southern armies from 1861-1865 reflected how the Irish population had grown dramatically between 1850 and 1860. By 1860, the Irish population was scattered across the South in large numbers and on both sides of the Mississippi River. Distinct Irish and Scotch-Irish communities were christened with names such as "Scotchville" in Georgia, "Belfast" in South Carolina, "Kinsale" in Virginia, and "San Patricio de Hibernia" in Texas.

Brig. Gen. James McIntosh (Resigned from the U.S. Army in 1861 and joined the Confederacy; killed at Pea Ridge, March 7, 1862; his brother fought for the Union

This large Irish contribution to the Confederate war effort has been overlooked partly because relatively few Irish generals served in the Confederacy. Only six of the 425 Confederate generals were Ireland-born: Patrick Ronayne Cleburne, William Montague Browne, Walter Paye Lane, Joseph Finegan, James Hagan, and Patrick Theodore Moore, though a few, including James McIntosh, were of Irish decent. One of the best examples of successful assimilation of the Irish in the South west of the Mississippi River was the case of Gen. Patrick Ronayne Cleburne, who was born in County Cork, Ireland. After leaving behind the "old country" as he called it,

2nd Lt. John B. McIntosh (fought for the Union while his brother was a general in the Confederate army

Cleburne became a successful lawyer in Helena, Arkansas. Here, the transplanted Irishman thrived in local social and political circles and he eventually became the only foreign-born major general of the Confederacy. During the ill-fated Tennessee invasion after the fall of Atlanta, the brilliant Irish division commander, who had acquired the reputation as the "Stonewall of the West," was killed in a doomed attack on the

Col. Joseph Finegan, Provisional Army of the CSA from Florida. (Enlisted 1861, survived)

fortifications of Franklin, Tennessee, on November 30, 1864. Tragically, Cleburne's wish came true in his fall on the battlefield of Franklin: he had repeatedly sworn that he preferred death to seeing the Confederacy's bid for independence crushed.

Among Gen. Robert E. Lee's officer corps of the Army of Northern Virginia were a larger number of Ireland-born colonels, the highest number of the army's foreign-born colonels. These colonels included: Peter Brennan (Sixty-first Georgia Infantry) who was killed at Gettysburg; William Giroud Burt (Twenty-second South Carolina Infantry); William Craig (Twentieth Georgia Infantry); John Dooley (First Virginia Infantry); the father-son team of Robert Emmet McMillan, Sr. and Robert Emmet McMillan, Jr. (both of the Twenty-fourth Georgia Infantry); Michael A. Grogan (Second Louisiana Infantry); Joseph Hamilton (Phillips' Georgia Legion); Joseph Hanlon (Sixth Louisiana Infantry); Michael Lynch (Twenty-first Georgia Infantry); William Monaghan (Sixth Louisiana Infantry) who was killed in August 1864; James Nelligan (First Louisiana Infantry);

Michael Nolan (First Louisiana Infantry) who was killed at Gettysburg; James Reilly (Rowan Artillery from North Carolina); Henry B. Strong (Sixth Louisiana Infantry) who was killed near the East Woods of Antietam; J. Moore Wilson (Seventh Louisiana Infantry); and other Irish leaders who were no less distinguished.

A far higher percentage of Irish served in the lower ranks of the Confederate Army. In the Tenth Louisiana Infantry, lieutenants Patrick Barron, Daniel Mahoney, and Michael Carroll were the only Ireland-born soldiers of the regiment to receive an officer's commission during the four years of Civil War.

James Hagan, one of six Confederate generals who were born in Ireland.

Large numbers of Irishmen also served in the Confederate Navy and the Southern merchant marine. A handful of Ireland-born soldiers transferred from the Tenth Louisiana Infantry to the famed C.S.S. *Virginia*: John Murphy, Patrick Noon, John Bregan, Michael Ellis, Edward Harrington, and Thomas Ripert. In many ways, the extensive contribution of the Irish in the Confederate Navy was comparable to the large percentage of African Americans who served in the Union Navy, a largely unrecognized and forgotten role.

The estimated 30,000 Irishmen who served in the ranks of southern armies represented only the number of Ireland-born Confederates.

Patrick Theodore Moore, commander of the First Virginia Infantry at First Bull Run, where he received a head wound.

William Montague Browne was a close friend of Jefferson Davis, and served in a variety of political and military positions during the war.

Walter Paye Lane fought in the Texas Revolution, the Mexican War and was a member of the Texas Rangers during the Republic years. He served in several Texas units during the Civil War and was severely wounded at the Battle of Mansfield.

The figure would have been far higher if the Scotch-Irish were included in this total. Indeed, by 1861, the central foundation of southern society, as first established during the colonial period and expanded farther inland during the course of western expansion throughout both the Eighteenth and Nineteenth Centuries, had Scotch-Irish roots in terms of culture, folk-ways, and population.

The memory of England's centuries of domination over Ireland provided both inspiration and lessons to the Irish population in the South in the spring of 1861. Many southern Irishmen felt that the South's struggle for self-determination was similar to Ireland's revolutionary efforts to shake off the yoke of British domination. Allowing yet another powerful centralized government to suppress an agrarian people of a largely rural society, in this case the infant Confederacy, would be reliving the failures of their Irish forefathers. To these men, the Confederacy's break from the Union was a mere continuation of the great Irish Revolution of 1798.

Irish revolutionary heritage revolved around repeated attempts to overthrow the subjugation of an entire people. Generation after generation, rebellions among the long-suffering people of Ireland were almost a regular feature of life in Ireland. The most famous

C.S.S. Virginia

of these Irish revolts included Owen Roe O'Neill's uprising in 1649; Patrick Sarsfield's rebellion in 1689; the Jacobite revolt in 1691; the great Irish Revolution of the summer of 1798 when more than 100,000 Irish rose up in opposition to the government; Robert Emmet's abortive insurrection in 1803; and the Young Ireland rebellion of 1848. All of these nationalist movements were doomed to failure. The Irish also blamed the 1840s horrors of the Great Famine upon the land and economic policies of the English rulers of Ireland.

Irish revolutionary heritage had a powerful affect on the emotions, psychology, and motivations of the Irishmen in gray. Not surprisingly, Capt. John Edward Dooley, First Virginia Infantry of Richmond, who was wounded and captured during the ill-fated "Pickett's Charge" at Gettysburg on

July 3, 1863, recorded an analogy between the Civil War and the failed Irish Revolution of 1798 in his journal: "Read today of fearful cruelties perpetuated by the English soldiers in '98 upon the Irish[.] Their fiendish acts upon defenseless people we find sometimes paralleled by the infamous brutalities of the

Patrick R. Cleburne was one of the most well-respected Irishmen in the South. He is commonly referred to as the "Stonewall of the West," and was killed at the Battle of Franklin.

Yankee mercenaries of the present day." Father John B. Bannon, the fiery, Ireland-born chaplain of the First Missouri Brigade, often described the Confederacy's struggle for nationhood as identical with that of Ireland because the 1861-1865 war—like Ireland's fight against the British—was a righteous, nationalist struggle for self-determination, or "Home Rule." John Mitchel, the Irish nationalist and revolutionary of the failed 1848 Young Ireland Nationalist movement, emphasized the certain "sort of parallel [existing] between the condition of the Southern states and that of Ireland," and that the South's ultimate solution "as in Ireland, is Repeal of the Union," or secession, and the winning of independence by way of violent revolution.

Inspired by the revolutionary struggles of the Irish against the British, these Irishmen in gray often went to war with emerald green flags emblazoned with the inspiring symbols of gold Irish harps—the banners of an independent Ireland and carried by generations of Irish revolutionaries— which were decorated with the Gaelic words of ancient Irish war cries and mottoes of the revolutionary past. Patrick R. Cleburne wrote in a letter the way many Irish across the South felt during this time: "The fever of revolution is very contagious." Some Irish Confederates even marched off to war in green uniforms.

The legacies and traditions of Ireland's revolutionary past served as a primary source of inspiration. A Tennessee newspaperman of the *Memphis Daily Appeal* on April 30, 1862, described how "when the banner of resistance to despotism was raised in the South, the generous, chivalrous Irishmen flocked to its fold, offering their lives in its defense. None are truer patriots—none are more willing to suffer martyrdom in freedom's cause than the oppressed sons of Erin's Isle . . . exiled from the land of his nativity by oppression." Irishmen across the South were "willing to render every possible assistance to a land struggling for that which Ireland attempted to obtain," but could never succeed against the overpowering military might of Great Britain.

Even though thousands of miles from their native land, the Confederate Irish also fought for a distinctive set of religious principles and their own religious beliefs rooted in the faith of the Irish peasants of the land: Catholicism. While Confederate leaders believed that the South was the last bastion of the true republican principles of the Founding Fathers, Father John B. Bannon, and other Confederate Irish, were convinced that the southern nation was the last true bastion of a strict interpretation of the utopian religious principles that had led to the establishment of a Christian nation in the New World. Irishmen in gray like Father Bannon believed that northern society and culture were morally corrupt by 1861. Bannon was convinced that the Union's real objectives were not in behalf of "such high-sounding and attractive sentiments as 'the old flag,' 'the Constitution,' and 'the union,'" but rather a Machiavellian design "to enrich the nation of Yankee manufacturers by the plunder of the farmers and planters of the South." Father Bannon viewed the industrialized, more progressive and liberal North as a serious threat not only to the conservative, agrarian South but also to the American republic's foundations, as envisioned by the Founding Fathers.

Bannon, called the "Fighting Chaplain" by the men of the First Missouri Confederate Brigade, attempted to gain the moral high ground for the Confederacy, which was lost with the 1862 Emancipation Proclamation. Bannon wrote a lengthy September 2, 1863, letter to Confederate Secretary of State Judah P. Benjamin to urge that an official letter should be written to the Pope in Rome by President Jefferson Davis to gain moral support for the beleaguered Confederacy and to perhaps open the door to foreign recognition. The Ireland-born chaplain described how Catholicism, as it existed in the South, was not only more conservative but also morally superior to the bankrupt and corrupt morality of northern liberalism and Protestantism: ". . . the conservative spirit & Catholic sentiments implanted in the country by the Catholic settlers of Maryland, Florida, the Gulf coast & old Louisiana from the mouth of the Misspi [*sic*] to the mouth of the Missouri Rivers [near St. Louis] & that the Southern people have been true to these [religious, moral, and conservative] principles, may be shown by their having uniformly spurned association with the infidel element imported from Revolutionary France & infidel Germany . . ." In the same letter, Father Bannon lamented how Catholicism had been "the victim of northern fanaticism [and] that Catholicity holds a far higher social position in the

Southern cities of Baltimore [Maryland], St. Louis, & New Orleans, than in any city of the northern states . . ."

Thanks to the lessons of Irish history, no people in the South responded to the call to strike a blow for southern independence with more enthusiasm than the Irish. While New Orleans contained the highest number of Irish, an estimated 25,000, by the time of the start of the Civil War, other Southern cities possessed sizeable numbers of Irish. The birthplace of secession, Charleston, South Carolina, was the southern Atlantic port that received the most Irish immigrants from 1815 to 1830 and contained approximately 3,200 Irish in 1860. During the antebellum period, many Irish served in militia units, such as the Irish Volunteers of Charleston. Sir William Howard Russell, a journalist educated at Trinity College in Dublin, Ireland, proudly maintained that "the Emerald Isle had contributed largely to the population of Charleston."

Pvt. Simon Fogarty, Co. F, First Regiment Charleston Guard (Enlisted 1863; survived)

Charleston's proudest company was known as the Old Irish Volunteers, one of the oldest militia companies in Charleston's history. Another Irish company from Charleston was the Meagher Guards, named in honor of Irish revolutionary Thomas Francis Meagher. When Meagher chose to fight for the Union and lead the Irish Brigade, the name of this Irish company was quickly changed to the Emerald Light Infantry. During the war years, the Confederate garrison of Fort Sumter consisted mostly of Irish soldiers of the Charleston Battalion.

With the call to arms, Emerald Islanders poured forth from Savannah, Georgia, where the Irish represented more than 22 percent of the total white population. The Irish Jasper Greens, named in honor of Sgt. William Jasper, the hero of Fort Moultrie who later died in the attack on Savannah during the American Revolution, was founded in 1843, recognized as one of the elite militia companies of Savannah. The Irish Jasper Greens consisted mostly of common laborers who enhanced their social status by enlisting in the military company. Savannah also produced two other Irish companies in the First Georgia Volunteers.

The Irish constituted more than 16 percent of the white population of Mobile, Alabama. One Southerner in that thriving port city never forgot the sight when the proud Irish soldiers of the Emerald Guards, Company I, Eighth Alabama Infantry, entrained for the Virginia theater. He described how "they were dressed in dark green, the emblematic color of Ireland, and carried a very beautiful flag, presented to them by some ladies. It was a Confederate flag on one side, in the center of which was a full length figure of [Gen. George] Washington; on the other side was the harp encircled with the wreath of shamrocks and the [Gaelic] words, 'Faugh-a-ballagh!' which means 'clear the way.'" Ironically, this legendary Gaelic war-cry was unleashed on the battlefield and painted on the battle-flags of General Meagher's Union warriors of the Irish Brigade.

Of the 109 soldiers in the ranks of Mobile's Emerald Guards, a total of 104 were born in Ireland. Capt. P. Loughry led the Emerald Guards with a great deal of Celtic pride in his company from the south Alabama port. Indicating that this war was a holy crusade for the Confederate Irish, Ireland-born John Quinlan, the bishop of Mobile, blessed the Irish battle-flag of the Emerald Guards. One company of Mobile Irish went to war specifically "in honor of Robert Emmet," who was executed by the British for his dream of an independent Ireland. Not surprisingly, largely Irish units, like the horsemen of the Mobile Dragoons, rode off to war from southern port cities on the Atlantic coast and along the coastal plains of the Gulf of Mexico.

Interior regions of southeastern states also formed distinctly Irish units as well. From central Alabama, a well-trained, disciplined prewar militia company known as the Irish Volunteers marched forth from the town of Montgomery. The Emerald Guards, led by Irish Capt. Bernard O'Connell, formed part of the Twenty-first Alabama Infantry. Company B of the Ninth Alabama Confederate Infantry was also an Irish company. Georgia contributed Irish companies such as the Irish Volunteers from Augusta, and the Jackson Guards (Company B) of the Nineteenth Georgia Infantry. A good many "Bluegrass Irishmen" from Kentucky served in the cavalry command of Gen. John Morgan, one of the most daring cavalry commanders of the Confederacy.

Irish communities, or culturally-distinct ethnic enclaves, thrived in major cities across the South, especially in the major ports along the Mississippi River. For instance, the "Irish Channel" district of New Orleans and "Kerry Patch" (named in honor of County Kerry in southwest Ireland) of north St. Louis were distinct Irish urban communities in the Mississippi Valley. As in Ireland, these neighborhoods centered around the Catholic church, and the working class Irish (mostly Catholic immigrants) lived in overcrowded boarding houses, dirty tenement slums, and rough shanty towns that were as Gaelic in cultural terms as Dublin, Cork, or Galway in Ireland.

While the percentage of volunteers among the South's Irish population was high ethnically, only 30,000 of the estimated 500,000 to 1,500,000 Confederate soldiers were Ireland-born. Immigrants from the lower and middle class districts of major southern cities volunteered for Confederate service in great numbers. Not surprisingly, one journalist of New Orleans wrote with some astonishment in the *Daily Delta* how: "As for our Irish citizens—whew!—they are 'spiling for a fight' with old Abe" Lincoln and his forces.

So many Irish New Orleaneans were eager to fight that efforts were made to create an Irish Brigade. As an enthusiastic *Daily Delta* reporter predicted on May 19, 1861: "we can vouch for 4,000 Irishmen in this city, ready and willing to enter the [Irish] Brigade and fight for the South to the cannon's mouth." But the ambitious dream of a Confederate Irish Brigade soon faded, with Irish companies instead serving as the nucleus for a number of Louisiana infantry regiments that organized in the spring and summer of 1861. One of these units, Company B (also known as the Calhoun Guards) of the Sixth Louisiana Infantry, contained 110 Ireland-born soldiers out of a total of 140 members.

Missouri possessed an Irish population of more than 43,000 in 1860. In St. Louis, many volunteers hailed from the lower working class Irish section of the city known as "Kerry Patch." Most residents of "Kerry Patch" were Catholics and recent immigrants from the Emerald Isle. An ethnic and cultural animosity existed between the Irish and the Germans in St. Louis, which erupted into an open feud in the spring of 1861. At that time, many Irish flocked to the ranks of the pro-southern Missouri State Guard and later into Confederate service. The Shamrock Guards was composed exclusively of Irish volunteers from St. Louis. The Germans, along with Irishmen who believed in the preservation of the Union, joined the Federal forces, producing a powder keg in the already combustable border state.

Sandwiched between St. Louis and New Orleans, the Mississippi River port city of Memphis, Tennessee, turned out large numbers of Irish volunteers for the Confederacy. Many of these men came from the Irish "Pinch District" of Memphis. In total, the Second Tennessee Confederate Infantry was composed of seven companies of Irish soldiers. Irishmen also volunteered in large numbers in the state capital of Nashville. Like the Tenth Tennessee Infantry Regiment of Volunteers (Irish), the Fifth Tennessee Confederate Infantry "was composed almost entirely of Irishmen."

Throughout the antebellum period, Irish families settled in the rural areas outside the major southern cities as well. The rural countryside of Louisiana, dominated by a large French population of around 5,000, also contained sizable numbers of Irish. Nearly 4,000 Irish people resided in the Louisiana countryside, and many of these Irishmen volunteered for Confederate service when war broke out. Of the 2,268 foreign-born Louisiana soldiers of "Lee's Tigers" of the Army of Northern Virginia, a total of 1,463 were Ireland-born Rebels, representing the highest number of any "foreign" nation in the ranks.

In the war's beginning, Irishman Col. P.B. O'Brien led a Louisiana militia regiment known as the Louisiana Irish Regiment, Volunteer State Troops Militia Infantry. The names of the companies of this Irish unit, such as the Shamrock Guards, invoked the sacred memory of old Ireland.

Pvt. William S. Callaway, Co. A, Ninth Louisiana Infantry.

Of the regiments of "Lee's Tigers" who fought with distinction under the blue Pelican Flag in the Army of Northern Virginia, many soldiers were born in Ireland: 202 in the First Louisiana Infantry which included all-Irish companies such as the Montgomery Guards and Emmet Guards; thirty-seven in the Second Louisiana Infantry; ninety-four in the Fifth Louisiana Infantry; 331 in the Seventh Louisiana Infantry which included a company known as the Irish Volunteers from Donaldsonville, Louisiana; 141 in the Eighth Louisiana Infantry; eighty-five in the Ninth Louisiana Infantry; and 118 in the Fifteenth Louisiana Infantry. Half of the companies of the Tenth Louisiana Infantry were Irish, while nearly as many (four companies), were Irish in the Twelfth Louisiana Infantry. Many Ireland-born Rebels also served in the Fourteenth Louisiana.

Reflecting Irish culture, tradition, and history, these Irish companies were christened with distinctive Irish names: the Emmet Guards and the Montgomery Guards (Companies D and E respectively) of the First Louisiana Infantry; the Sarsfield Rangers of Company C, Fifth Louisiana Infantry; and the Irish Volunteer Company of the Seventh Louisiana Infantry. Two companies, F and I, of the Seventh Louisiana

Infantry were Irish units. More than one-third of the soldiers of the Seventh Louisiana were born in Ireland.

The Louisiana regiment of the Army of Northern Virginia which contained the highest number of Irish was the Sixth Louisiana Infantry. Seven of its ten companies contained immigrant Irish from New Orleans, a city which provided more Irish soldiers than any other in the South. This infantry regiment was so thoroughly Irish that it was also known as "the South's Irish Brigade," containing mostly Irish Catholic immigrants. A total of 468 Sixth Louisiana soldiers, primarily laborers and other menial workers from the thriving city of New Orleans and recruited largely from the uneducated, lower working class immigrants, were Ireland-born. These unruly Irishmen were known as "the wharf rats from New Orleans," because they gained a reputation for ferocity not only on, but also off the battlefield.

The reputation for rioting, thievery, looting, and hell-raising of the Louisiana "Tigers" became legendary across the Confederacy. Some soldiers went to war with hat bands proclaiming "Tiger in Search of Abe." One Virginia soldier described them as "the most rakish and devilish looking beings I ever saw." In the war's beginning, even the journey to the Virginia theater by rail provided an opportunity for the Louisiana Rebels to enhance their reputations for troublemaking. The trip across the South included drunkenness, nine deaths, a rash of shootings, a seemingly endless number of fist fights, the brazen high-jacking of a train by the enlisted men to escape their officers, physical abuse of citizens along the way, the pillaging of stores and private houses, and more.

A tough Irish-American soldier of the Fifteenth Alabama Infantry, Cpl. William A. McClendon, described Lee's "Louisiana Tigers" as "all Irish . . . and tigers they were too in human form. I was actually afraid of them [but] they were brave, desperate fighters . . ." In a June 1863 letter, a Georgia Rebel described the Louisiana "Tigers" as " . . . perfect 'devils' and [Capt. O.P. Miller who led the Old Dominion Guards of Maj. Roberdeau Wheat's Louisiana Battalion from New Orleans] was the only man who could control them, which he did by cursing, beating and shooting them when they disobeyed him." On one occasion after Miller learned that his soldiers were holed up in a private residence, "he ordered his men to [their] camps, saying if they did not leave he would kill them." When a lieutenant answered defiantly, Miller "struck him over the head several times with his pistol." Later, the Louisiana "Tigers" returned to the house, and Captain Miller again ordered the men back to camp, but this time he was shot in the back and killed by his own soldiers.

Col. William Calvin Oates, the Scotch-Irish commander of the Fifteenth Alabama during the struggle for possession of Little Round Top on July 2, 1863, referred to the wild Louisiana Irish as members of "Wheat's notorious 'Tiger' battalion." A hard-nosed individualist who had led an adventurous life across the southwestern frontier before settling down in his native Alabama, Colonel Oates also described how the "Tigers" were "composed mainly of adventurers, wharf-rats, cut-throats, and bad characters generally; and although they fought with reckless bravery so long as their organization continued, they were actuated more by a spirit of adventure and love of plunder than by love of country." Oates continued, "no one could command or control them [and] . . . they had no moral principle whatever, but fought like devils . . ."

Perhaps no Confederate regiment could boast of more high-ranking Ireland-born officers than the Sixth Louisiana. Colonels Henry B. Strong, William Monaghan, and Lt. Col. Joseph Hanlon all commanded the Sixth Louisiana at one time or other during the war. In addition, the adjutant of the regiment, John Orr, was Ireland-born. Both colonels Strong and Monaghan were killed while leading their troops in the heat of battle.

The Irish who fought for the Confederacy were not only from New Orleans, but from lands west of the Mississippi River. The Shamrock Guards joined the struggle to defend Missouri from Union invasion in the war's beginning. The sons and grandsons of the Texas Revolution, including those from San Patricio de Hibernia (an Irish colony established in the early 1830s) flocked into the ranks of Irish units across Texas. Hard-fighting Irish Rebels served in Gen. John B. Hood's famed Texas Brigade, one of the elite combat units of the Civil War. A good many Irish marched off to war from the distinctive Irish community known as the Irish Flats in San Antonio.

The Irish of Paulding, Mississippi, united to form the Jasper Grays. Many Irishmen served in the ranks of the Mississippi Brigade, Army of Northern Virginia, under Gen. William Barksdale who was killed on July 2, 1863, at Gettysburg. Large numbers of Irishmen filled the ranks of Mississippi companies and regiments from across the state. Indeed, "it was rare in the Mississippi companies not to find at least one Irishman."

One key reason why the Confederate Irish fought so determinedly on the battlefield was in part because they felt that they were representatives of their homeland. As a result of compensating for prejudice and negative stereotypes that placed a blemish on the Irish character, the Irish Rebels often fought more courageously—or more recklessly—than their non-Irish counterparts: a fact noted with regularity in Confederate memoirs and recollections. In the words of one Southerner, Irish soldiers wearing the gray battled tenaciously for "the honor and glory of that 'green isle of the sea.'"

From the beginning to the war's end, the combat prowess of the Irish Confederates rose to legendary heights across the South. As an indication of this fact, the Confederate Irish were often the most fierce fighters, and suffered the highest and disproportionate number of casualties. The well-known fighting prowess of the Irish soldier was evident when the Confederate War Department, with considerable insight, advised that "Catholic Irish be preferred," when converting Union prisoners into Confederate soldiers upon exchange.

As much as their hard-fighting qualities, examples of hot Irish tempers and the legendary pungency of the Confederate Irish appear often in Confederate accounts. The outspokenness, clever wit, and spunky nature of the average Irish Confederate was especially evident during defiant confrontations of privates with company, regiment, and brigade commanders. For example, when brigade commander Gen. John Stevens Bowen was approached by a ragged Irish soldier who complained about not receiving rations during a dreary withdrawal after yet another Confederate defeat at Corinth, Mississippi, in early October 1862, the Georgia general merely replied, "Why, my man, did you not get plenty of corn and pumpkin [from the fields] last night?" The disgruntled Irishman responded with a blunt remark that was as sarcastic as it was bitter: "Sure, Gineral, do you think I am a horse?"

Sgt. William Henry Andrews, First Georgia Regulars, Army of Northern Virginia, described in his postwar memoir entitled *Footprints of a Regiment* how, "we have a good many Irish in the regiment, and while they are good hardy soldiers, they are hard to control. [For] they will have their dram if it is to be had, and they can find it where no one else will look for it [and] the boys have fights in camps pretty often [but] the Georgia boys are no match for the Irish laddie with his fist, so have to resort to some kind of weapon to defend themselves . . ."

Lt. Col. Robert S. Bevier, an aristocratic and well-educated lawyer from Macon, Missouri, described the paradox of the elite Irish soldiery of the First Missouri Confederate Brigade, which was one of the best combat brigades in the West in no small part because of the large number of Irish in the ranks. He wrote how he "had two Irish [companies] in my command; the best soldiers on duty and the worst off, the best fighters and the most troublesome men in the army . . . one evening I heard a rumpus in the camp, and on going to it found a couple of Irishmen engaged in a pugilistic encounter over a stick of wood . . ." So many Irish served in the Missouri Brigade that some soldiers called it the "Irish Brigade." In the heat of battle, the Missouri Irish in gray often charged forward with the battle-cry, "At them boys! at them! for the honour of old Ireland."

The faithful chaplain of the Missouri Brigade, Father John B. Bannon, left his new Catholic church in St. Louis at the request of the Irish soldiers because they were without a priest in Gen. Sterling Price's Missouri State Guard in the first year of war. More than once, the six foot, four inch Father Bannon intervened to physically break up fist-fights among his Irish flock.

In general, the Irish Confederate soldiers fought best when they served together in distinctive Irish companies and regiments. This development in part resulted from the fact that the Confederate Irish fought not only for each other, but also for the dream of independence of an infant nation and for the honor of Ireland. Throughout the war years, these were powerful motivations for the Irish Confederates in the ranks. Indeed, from 1861 to 1865, "the green flag seemed to exert a magnetic control over the brawny sons of the Emerald Isle. Their fondness for their own companies is explicable: the Irishman fights better shoulder to shoulder with Irishmen as comrades, and always yearns to reflect honor on 'Ould Ireland.'"

Quite simply, Irish solders repeatedly demonstrated that they were the hardest and most tenacious fighters in the Confederacy, a widely-recognized fact throughout the South. For instance, one veteran Confederate general who had a reputation as a hard fighting, aggressive commander, understood with clarity exactly what was often the key to Confederate success on the battlefield: "If tomorrow I wanted to win a reputation, I would have Irish soldiers in preference to any other[.] First, they have more dash, more elan than any other troops that I know of; then they are more cheerful and enduring—nothing can depress them[.] Not only cheerful, but they were submissive to discipline when once broken in—and where they had good officers their attachment to them was unbounded. And confidence was established the moment they saw their general in the fight with them[.] [I]f I had to take from one to 10,000 men to make a reputation with, I'd take the same men as I had in the war—Irishmen from the city, the levees, the river, the railroads, the canals, or from ditching and fencing on the plantations[.] They make the finest soldiers that ever shouldered a musket." Gen. Richard Taylor, who commanded "Lee's Tigers" of Louisiana, marveled how the Irish Confederates "follow their officers to the death." One Southerner recalled that the Confederate Irish were always "in the foremost ranks of battle" no matter how severe the fighting or how impossible the odds. And another Confederate described how the Irish in gray amid the heat of combat always seemed eager "to give his life and fortunes to a cause he loved."

In the many bloody battles across the Eastern Theater under Stonewall Jackson in the Shenandoah Valley of Virginia, the Louisiana "Tigers" were repeatedly employed as shock troops during some of the fiercest battles of the war. Again and again, it was Lee's dependable "Tigers" who rose to the challenge, leading a frontal or flank attack, holding a key defensive position, or protecting a risky withdrawal. In the process, these Celtic warriors from Louisianna compiled one of the most distinguished combat records in the Army of Northern Virginia.

One of the typical Irish Confederate soldiers who rose to the challenge on the battlefield was described by Maj. Robert

Stiles in his *Four Years Under Marse Robert*: "an Irishman named Burgoyne in the Ninth Louisiana [who was] a typical son of the Emerald Isle, over six feet high in his stockings (when he had any), broad-shouldered and muscular, slightly bow-legged, and springy as a cat; as full of fire and fight and fun as he could hold . . ." Major Stiles, an aristocratic Virginian cavalier, also wrote of a Georgia artillery unit, which "was composed of Irishmen from Savannah—gallant fellows, but wild and reckless." Such descriptions of the Irish warriors in gray were so widespread in contemporary and postwar Confederate accounts as to seem almost stereotypical, but nevertheless, were based on historical fact.

Another feature of the Confederate Irish that appeared repeatedly in Confederate letters, memoirs, and reminiscences was their distinctive brand of Irish humor, especially in the face of adversity or against impossible odds. Perhaps one of the best representative examples of the well-known sarcastic, gallows humor of the common Irish soldier occurred immediately before the charge of the Missouri Brigade at Franklin, Tennessee. Here, when Gen. John B. Hood's Army of Tennessee sought to destroy Gen. John Schofield's forces before they escaped north to the safety of Nashville, Tennessee, the exiled command of Missouri Confederates was destined to suffer the highest loss of any brigade in the war, nearly 70 percent. The Missouri Brigade lost at least 419 of 696 attackers, including the commander of the Third and Fifth Missouri Infantry (Consolidated) Ireland-born Capt. Patrick Canniff. This promising twenty-four-year-old saddle-maker from St. Louis was killed along with a good many other Irishmen of the Missouri Brigade at the battle of Franklin,

Tennessee. As the Missouri Brigade was about to launch its ill-fated, suicidal attack upon the strong fortifications of Franklin, the nervous tension was high among the ranks of these hardened veterans of the Missouri "Old Guard." When one common soldier quoted Admiral Horatio Nelson's famous 1805 Trafalgar order that, "England expects every man to do his duty," a St. Louis Irishman of the First and Fourth Missouri Infantry (Consolidated) responded with a laugh: "It's damn little duty England would get out of this Irish crowd." As so often in the past, the Irishmen in gray displayed their high spirits and high morale by "laughing in the face of death" before a difficult attack.

An analysis of the best combat units in both the Eastern and Western Theaters during some of the war's most decisive battles reveals that it was the Irish soldier or regiment that most often rose to the fore, either leading an attack or bolstering a defensive stand, inspiring other troops or in protecting a withdrawal as an army's reliable guardians. Most important, these timely contributions were made by the Confederate Irish often when an important battle hung in the balance.

Some of the best examples of these sterling combat qualities can be found in the performance of the Irish of Company K, Fifteenth Alabama, in the struggle to capture Little Round Top at Gettysburg on July 2, 1863; the Irish of the First Missouri Brigade during the decisive clash of the Vicksburg campaign at Champion Hill, Mississippi, and then during the assault on Franklin, Tennessee, on November 30, 1864; Lt. Richard "Dick" Dowling's Irish soldiers who stopped a mighty Union invasion at Sabine Pass, Texas, on September 8, 1863;

an Irish lieutenant of the "Irish Battalion" inspiring his men to hold firm against Union assults when defending the railroad embankment at Second Manassas at the end of August 1862, by crushing the head of a Union attacker with a rock when ammunition had been expended; and a host of other examples of overcoming adversity.

But earning the reputation as the most tenacious and hardest fighting troops of the Confederacy came at a frightful price. The best and brightest of the Confederate Irish were left on the battlefields across the South and beyond at Antietam and Gettysburg. The Louisiana regiment most completely dominated by Ireland-born soldiers, the Sixth Louisiana Infantry, counted only a handful of soldiers left in its decimated ranks by the time of its surrender at Appomattox Court House, Virginia, on April 9, 1865. Among the few survivors—only fifty-two men—were Irishmen such as nineteen-year-old Tommy Cavanaugh, who had enlisted at age fifteen in New Orleans as a drummer boy; two veterans with the same name, Patrick Murphy; and an Ireland-born sailor, James Donovan. These were the lucky Confederate Irish survivors of the Sixth Louisiana, who had left many of their Ireland-born comrades killed, maimed, or captured on the battlefield. The experiences of Cavanaugh, Donovan, and the two Patrick Murphys were representative of the tragic fate of most Confederate Irish, who fought against their fellow countrymen, both Northerners and Irishmen, for what they believed was right.

The following representative examples will focus on the prominent role that Confederate Irish troops played in key situations—or decisive turning points—during some of the most important battles of the Civil War, with an added emphasis upon those confrontations that pitted Irishmen in blue against Irishmen in gray to provide a unique perspective of the Civil War among the Irish people in America, within the larger national conflict of civil war.

Not long after the end of the nightmare of the Civil War, a member of the British Parliament from Ireland, John Francis Maguire, made the following keen observation in regard to the brothers' war between the Irish from 1861 to 1865 and the tragic fate of the Irish in both the North and South: "the Southern Irishman could not reconcile it to his notions of consistency, that the very men [Irishmen in blue] who sought to liberate their native land from British thralldom should join with those who were doing their utmost to subjugate and trample under foot the liberties of a people fighting for their independence," and a new infant nation, the Confederacy.

Dr. Phillip Thomas Tucker
Washington, D.C.

CHAPTER 1

The Irish Rebels of the Tenth Louisiana Clash with the Irish Brigade at Malvern Hill, July 1, 1862

In 1982, two respected scholars, Dr. Grady McWhiney and Dr. Perry D. Jamieson, produced the ground-breaking book, *Attack and Die: Civil War Military Tactics and the Southern Heritage.* The central thesis of this work was that the Confederacy bled itself to death by an over-reliance on the tactical offensive in part because of the successful offensive lessons of the Mexican War, before advances in weaponry—primarily the rifled musket—made those offensive tactics largely obsolete. This work maintained that the Southerners' heavy reliance on the tactical offensive throughout the war resulted from the cultural and historical legacy of a Celtic past. For centuries, Celtic warriors were not only noted for their ferocity in combat but also for their over-reliance on offensive warfare, regardless of the odds or situation.

In many ways, this thesis provided an expla-
nation for Confederate defeat and why so little
remained of the Army of the Northern Virginia
when Gen. Robert E. Lee surrendered at
Appomattox Court House on Palm Sunday 1865.
From 1862-1865, that army—once considered
invincible—had been largely destroyed by Lee's
over-reliance upon the tactical offensive which
proved far too costly for the South's limited manpower. One of the best examples of the validity
of the "attack and die" thesis as expounded by
McWhiney and Jamieson was first demonstrated
in full at Malvern Hill, Virginia, on July 1, 1862.
Because of Lee's over-reliance of the tactical
offensive that resulted in repeated assaults
against a strong defensive position, this battle
was described by one Confederate general as
simply "murder."

*Thomas Francis Meagher
actively opposed Great
Britain's rule over Ireland, and
was exiled to Tasmania in
1849. He immigrated to the
United States in 1852 and settled in New York. He led the
Union's Irish Brigade until
May 14, 1863, when he
resigned his commission
because of political reasons.*

After the wounding of Gen. Joseph E.
Johnston at Seven Pines, Lee took command of
the Army of Northern Virginia. He immediately
took the offensive, attacking Gen. George B. McClellan's
Army of the Potomac at seemingly every opportunity.
Unleashing blow after blow, the Confederate forces drove the
Union troops from the gates of Richmond and back down the
Virginia Peninsula.

By the end of June 1862, the Confederates had successfully pushed the Federals all the way back to the James
River, where the Army of the Potomac, after withdrawing to
the muddy James where Union warships offered protection,

aligned its vast arsenal of cannon along the high ground of Malvern Hill. In the retreat from Richmond, the dependable Federal unit that brought up and protected the retiring Union army's rear was the Irish Brigade. This Celtic unit contained the grand-nephew of martyred Irish revolutionary Robert Emmet, who had inspired so many Confederate Irish to cast their fate with the South. Here, on Malvern Hill, the weary, bloodied Union army made its last stand on commanding high ground with its back to the James River, while Federal gunboats in the river provided fire support. Convinced that McClellan's army could be destroyed, Lee unleashed his greatest offensive strike of the bloody Seven Days fighting. But Lee committed the ultimate folly of launching a tactical offensive against a strong natural position lined with most of the Union army's artillery along the crest of Malvern Hill.

Nevertheless, the lengthy formations of Rebels surged toward Malvern Hill with flags waving and bayonets sparkling in the early July sunshine. Lee and his men were confident of success and believed that they were about to win *the* decisive battle of the war. One of the attacking regiments of Lee's army was the Tenth Louisiana Confederate Infantry. This fine regiment contained a large percentage of Irish Rebels, who now charged forward with characteristic Celtic abandon and ancient Gaelic war-cries.

Most of these Emerald Island soldiers were laborers from the wharfs and docks of New Orleans, where before the war they loaded and unloaded steamboats along the busy levee. By 1860, New Orleans contained the largest Irish population in the South. From beginning to end, these New Orleans Celtic Rebels served with distinction in the Tenth Louisiana.

The Tenth Louisiana's ranks included many Irishmen: sixty-three in Company A, the Shepherd Guards; twelve in Company B, the Derbigry Guards; seventy-one in Company C, the Hewitt's Guards; forty-one in Company D, the Hawkins Guards; twelve in Company E, the Louisiana Swamp Rifles from Pointe Coupee, Louisiana; eight in Company G, the Orleans Rangers; thirty in Company H, the Orleans Blues; nine in Company K, the Confederate States Rangers from the swampy lowlands around St. Landry, Louisiana; and a scattering of Irish in other Tenth Louisiana companies as well.

As was the case in so many regiments in which Irish Confederates served, the Irish of the Tenth Louisiana were considered to be the best and hardest fighters in the unit. A close analysis at the total number of Tenth Louisiana Irish who fell on the battlefield throughout the unit's history indicated that the combativeness of the Confederate Irish was more fact than myth. Indeed, while the percentage of Irish who served in the Tenth Louisiana's ranks equaled 26 percent, they nevertheless accounted for over a full third of the total number of regimental battlefield losses—killed and wounded—during the war. Even more revealing was the fact that the Irish accounted for a total of 36 percent of the Tenth Louisiana's total number of battlefield fatalities. In summary, barely one-fourth of the regiment—the Irish—suffered 36 percent of the unit's fatalities.

Across the grassy slope of Malvern Hill, Lee's brigades continued to roll forward under a deadly hail storm of shot and shell, which poured forth from dozens of Federal cannons. In the late afternoon, the Tenth Louisiana surged into the leaden storm with the Virginia, Georgia, and Louisiana brigade under the command of Gen. Paul Jones Semmes, part of Gen. Lafayette McLaws' Division of Gen. John Bankhead Magruder's right wing, Army of Northern Virginia. Semmes's brigade swept wide across the rolling fields of the Crews farm to strike the left of McClellan's defensive line in an attempt to capture the roaring Union cannon dominating the high ground.

When the Federal V Corps on the left found itself in trouble while fighting against Lee's furious assaults, four regiments of the Union Irish Brigade were dispatched to bolster the weakening flank. During the advance, the Irishmen in blue clashed head-on with an advancing Confederate line. The spirited soldiers of the Eighty-eighth and Sixty-ninth New York attacked the Confederates with flashing bayonets and Celtic war-cries amid the smoke-laced woodlands.

To counter the Irish Brigade's success in pushing back the foremost Confederates, the Tenth Louisiana then launched an attack, striking the Irish Brigade troops a tremendous blow. Another savage flurry of close combat resulted, with Irishmen in blue exchanging bayonet thrusts and clubbed muskets with Emerald Islanders in gray, while unleashing with "a half-Gaelic, half-English scream." One Irish Brigade member wrote after the battle, "the color-sergeant flaunts the flags at the [Irish] rebels and falls . . . men brain and bayonet one another." It was reported that a Confederate colonel exclaimed, "Steady, boys here comes that damn green flag again!"

Here, amid the surreal slaughter at Malvern Hill, the Tenth Louisiana proved to be especially tough opponents for

Harper's Weekly *sketch of the Battle of Malvern Hill as it appeared in the July 26, 1862 issue.*

the Irishmen in blue. Without time to reload muskets, the Louisiana boys swung musket-butts and slashed with Bowie knives, while the Irish Brigade soldiers, who had no time to fix bayonets, smashed Confederate heads with the ends of their weapons. An Irishman of Company H (the Orleans Blues), of the Tenth Louisiana, thirty-year-old Pvt. Daniel Dean, a laborer from New Orleans, was almost bayoneted in the throat, but Lt. Col. Eugene Waggaman, commanding officer of the Tenth Louisiana, knocked the Irish Yankee's musket away at the last moment with his saber. A grim testimony to the savage fighting was evident from the large number of the New Yorkers' muskets with stocks shattered from crashing over Rebel heads. Losses were high among the Irish during the bloody melee. Some Ireland-born soldiers of the Tenth Louisiana killed in the battle included John McGee,

Charles McGill, Jerry Gordon, John Higgins, William Donovan, Andrew Roach, and John Mangan. Another sixteen were killed, and nine captured by the men of Meagher's Irish Brigade.

As darkness finally fell on bloody Malvern Hill, the savage fighting continued. One Irish Brigade soldier, Pvt. Richard Kelly of the Sixty-Ninth New York, reached up and pulled Lieutenant Colonel Waggaman off his horse and captured the "Tiger" leader. The Tenth Louisiana's fighting spirit dwindled with the capture of their leader, and the hard-hit Rebels finally withdrew.

On this day, Lee's badly-punished army sustained its worst defeat of the Seven Days battles. Perhaps the best testament to the fighting prowess of the Confederate Irish of the Tenth Louisiana was the fact that the Ireland-born soldiers accounted for nearly one-half of the regiment's losses at Malvern Hill, where Irishman from both sides met in a bloody reunion on July 1, 1862.

Irish Confederates from Georgia Helped Defend Burnside's Bridge at Antietam, September 17, 1862

During the late summer of 1862, Gen. Robert E. Lee and the Army of Northern Virginia embarked upon a desperate attempt to reverse the fortunes of war. Lee led his army northward from the depths of Virginia, across the Potomac River, and into western Maryland in a bold invasion of the North during the first week of September. This was the first northern invasion by Lee's Army of Northern Virginia. But this thrust north was ill-fated.

Thousands of veteran Confederates swarmed onto the soil of "My Maryland," after wading across the cold waters of the shallow Potomac. Knowing that he was on the losing end of a war of attrition, Lee needed to win a decisive victory on northern soil to fulfill the great dream of his fledgling nation's

Burnside's Bridge, where the Irishmen of the Twentieth Georgia repulsed Union attacks during the Battle of Antietam.

independence with official recognition from France and Great Britain. Thanks in part to the discovery of a copy of General Lee's campaign orders that fell into Union hands at Frederick, Maryland, Gen. George B. McClellan closed in on the Army of Northern Virginia, which had divided in widely-separated columns to capture Harpers Ferry, Virginia. Deciding to make a bold stand amid the fertile farmlands of western Maryland, Lee hurriedly concentrated his forces around a small Maryland town called Sharpsburg.

Here, behind the waters of Antietam Creek, a relative handful of Rebel units took position to met the rapidly-advancing Army of the Potomac. They made a defensive stand out of necessity to buy time for the arrival of the far-flung elements of Lee's scattered army. One battle-hardened command that took a key defensive position on the army's far right was a hard-fighting Georgia brigade under cantankerous and feisty Gen. Robert Augustus Toombs, a Georgia politician. Toombs had almost become the Confederacy's president until a wild, premature victory celebration turned into a drunken spree in the streets of Montgomery, Alabama, the night before the final balloting.

Toombs and his top lieutenant, Col. Henry Lewis Benning, who had won fame for his leadership abilities and battlefield accomplishments that earned him the sobriquet of "Old Rock," deployed their Georgia soldiers on the bluff overlooking a stately stone bridge, the Rohrbach Bridge. Most important, the Georgia Rebels, including a good many Irish, now occupied the best defensive terrain on the Antietam battlefield.

Robert Augustus Toombs was a Georgia politician who served as the Confederacy's first Secretary of State. He commanded the Twentieth Georgia during the Battle of Antietam.

This graceful stone bridge, dominated by three majestic arches, became known as "Burnside's Bridge." A distinctive architectural landmark in Washington County, Maryland, the limestone bridge was constructed in 1836 along the National Road. It linked the East with the productive lands of the Ohio and Mississippi Valley and accelerated internal development during the Jacksonian Period. The Rohrbach Bridge, also known as the Lower Bridge because it was the last stone bridge along Antietam Creek before it entered the Potomac River to the south, was not built with slave labor, even though Maryland was a slave state. Instead, the stone bridge had been erected by craftsmen, artisans, masons, and laborers from Ireland. When a cholera epidemic struck the community, hundreds of workmen died, sending many immigrant Irish to early graves in the soil of Washington County, Maryland.

Most Irish Confederates of Toombs's brigade, who served primarily in the Second and Twentieth Georgia Infantry, did not realize this fact, however. Among these two veteran regiments, most Irish Rebels served in the ranks of the Twentieth Georgia. Ireland-born Capt. William Craig, a merchant from Augusta, Georgia, led the Montgomery Guards, or Company K, of the Twentieth Georgia. This company was named for the Irish revolutionary, Gen. Richard Montgomery (killed in December 1775 while leading the attack on Quebec, Canada), and was organized in Richmond County, Georgia. The thirty-three-year-old Craig earned a promotion to major in early May 1864. Occasionally commanding the regiment, this capable Irish leader survived the war.

Two other companies aligned close to Company K at Antietam Creek—companies A and G of the Twentieth Georgia. Irishmen such as privates John O. Riley, Peter McIntyre, and Lee R. Hennegan served in the ranks of Company A, the Sparks Guards, who hailed from Macon, Georgia. Even more Irish soldiers served in Company G, many of whom came from the busy river port of Columbus, the largest city in the Chattahoochee River Valley. This elite Muscogee County company included privates James McCorkle, William McElrath, and Joseph M. McMillan in its list of Irishmen.

The terrain that overlooked Antietam Creek and the Rohrbach Bridge suited a defensive stand. The troops of companies A, G, and K of the Twentieth Georgia positioned themselves on the high ground immediately north of the bridge and to the left of the Second Georgia, situated south of the bridge. On the morning of September 17, Union Gen. Ambrose E. Burnside and Gen. Jacob D. Cox, who exercised tactical control of the sector before the stone bridge, unleashed the troops of the veteran IX Corps. Despite the pounding of IX Corps artillery and the repeated attacks by one Union regiment after another, the Georgians under the effective leadership team of Toombs and Benning held firm against the onslaught. The Confederate units suffered high losses in the defense, but stubbornly refused to budge under the heavy pressure.

Captain Craig and Company K along with the Second Georgia and the rest of the Twentieth Georgia, fired continuously until ammunition began to run low. In desperation, soldiers took rounds from the cartridge-boxes of the increasing number of dead and wounded who lay around them. For hours, the murderous hail of Georgia musketry streamed down from the commanding bluffs overlooking the Antietam, cutting down the attackers in blue. In a running gauntlet of fire, more Federals surged across the level bottom lands on the east side of the creek that led to the Antietam and the stone bridge. A number of Georgia Irishmen died in defense of the little stone bridge that had been erected by their countrymen many years before. The greatest irony, however, in the struggle for possession of the little stone bridge was that now some Irishmen in gray shot down advancing Irishmen in blue from the IX Corps. As in the clash between the Irish of the Tenth Louisiana and Meagher's Irish Brigade at Malvern Hill, the bloody contest for possession of the Rohrbach Bridge was yet another example of the horor of the civil war among the Irish in America.

By the late morning of September 17, it remained crucial for the survival of the Army of Northern Virginia that the Georgia troops continue to hold firm to the high ground perch overlooking Antietam Creek. Lee's army—decimated by desertion, straggling, and disease during the long march into Maryland—was now a mere skeleton of its former self. Under the overwhelming might of the Army of the Potomac, Lee's embattled Army of Northern Virginia was on the ropes by mid-day on September 17. By this time no Confederate sector was more vulnerable or weaker than Lee's far right flank, where less than 300 Georgians somehow held the line against the repeated blows of the IX Corps and concentrated fires of artillery and musketry, hour after hour. As Col. Edward Porter Alexander recorded in his personal recollections *Fighting For the Confederacy*, "Toombs with only [a relative handful of Georgia] men . . . save[d] the battle" of Antietam on decisive September 17, 1862.

With the life of Lee's army at stake, the Georgians protected not only the army's right flank but also its rear. If this band of Georgia defenders were pushed aside, then the mighty IX Corps would advance to capture a lightly-defended Sharpsburg. Such a success would result in McClellan's forces closing in on Lee's rear, while cutting off the Confederate army's avenue of withdrawal southward across the Potomac and out of western Maryland to Virginia's safety. As it was, only a small number of Georgia troops stood firm between the Army of the Potomac and the destruction of Lee's army.

Finally, at 1:30 P.M. on this scorching hot afternoon, the hard-fighting Georgians, after suffering more than 50 percent casualties, ran out of ammunition and were forced to withdraw. This extraction allowed the IX Corps to resume its offensive effort to capture the Rohrbach Bridge. In addition, a Federal division outflanked the Georgia troops from the south. This flank maneuver allowed hundreds of Union soldiers to attack the bridge defenders' vulnerable right flank, while they still faced Federals in their front.

Nevertheless, in thwarting McClellan's ambitions throughout the morning and early afternoon of September 17, the precious hours purchased by the Georgia troops kept the powerful IX Corps at bay and bought much needed time for the Army of Northern Virginia at Antietam. The defenders of the Second and Twentieth Georgia, including the many Irish Confederates, rose to the challenge of defending Burnside's Bridge "with a coolness and tenacity unsurpassed in [the] history" of the war.

The Union victory at Antietam ended the last hope for the Confederacy to gain foreign recognition from Great Britain or France. Irishman Thomas Conolly, from one of Ireland's leading families, watched the death throes of the Confederacy after the fall of Petersburg and Richmond, Virginia. He wrote in late April 1865: "I am very angry with England [and] France & the whole European world[.] Why did they not help the noble Confederates, that a gallant resistance against such fearful odds, this war has been comparatively a skeleton fighting against a giant." The Confederacy's fate was sealed with the Union success at Antietam, despite the best efforts and high sacrifice of the soldiers of the Army of Northern Virginia, including the Irishmen of companies A, G, and K, Twentieth Georgia.

CHAPTER 3

The Celtic-Gaelic Brothers' War: The Twenty-fourth Georgia Meets the Irish Brigade at Fredericksburg

The state of Georgia contributed hundreds of Irishmen to the Confederacy. The large, prosperous state provided Irishmen for two companies of the Emmet Rifles, along with units such as the Irish Volunteers (an antebellum militia company), the Irish Volunteer Guards of the Eighth Georgia Infantry, the Irish Jasper Greens of Savannah, Georgia, the Montgomery Guards, the Montgomery Sharpshooters of the Sixty-first Georgia Infantry, and the Montgomery Volunteers. In addition, a south central Georgia company known as the Telfair Irish Greys from Telfair County, Georgia, served in the ranks of the Twenty-fifth Georgia Infantry. One disgruntled non-Irish Protestant soldier stated in a November 1863 letter: "we are under Gen [Hugh Weedon] Mercer's command at

Savannah, Georgia, my Battalion is nearly all Irish and I want to get from among them."

As is evident in the name of the Irish Jasper Greens of Savannah, one of the leading revolutionary influences of the Georgia Rebels was Sgt. William Jasper. During the American Revolution, the diminutive Irishman jumped atop the parapet of Fort Moultrie during a fierce bombardment from the British naval fleet to replace the fallen flag of the Palmetto State during the defense of Charleston, South Carolina, on June 28, 1776. Sergeant Jasper's influence was so inspirational that Irishmen rallied to the ranks of the Irish Jasper Greens, a "crack militia company" in antebellum Savannah. The Irish Jasper Greens became Company A of the First Georgia Regulars, Army of Northern Virginia. Commanding the company was Capt. John Flannery who was born in County Tipperary, Ireland, and had come to Charleston, South Carolina, in 1851. He moved to Savannah three years later, then became commander of the Irish Jasper Greens. Like so many of their comrades, these Celtic-Gaelic soldiers fought under the green banner of old Ireland.

Pvt. Charles W.D. McHugh, Co. F, Twenty-fourth Georgia Infantry (Enlisted 1861, captured 1862, exchanged and survived)

Considered one of the best regiments of Lee's Army of Northern Virginia both in terms of drill field perfection and fighting prowess, the First Georgia Regulars contained a high percentage of Irish. In the words of Sgt. William Henry Andrews, First Georgia Regulars: "we have a good many Irish in the regiment, and while they are good [and] hardy soldiers, they are hard to control."

Perhaps the best example of the brothers' war among the Irish people in America took place on the gory field of Fredericksburg. Here the Twenty-fourth Georgia Infantry, which contained Irishmen from Hall, White, Gwinnett, Towns, Banks, and Elbert counties, met Thomas F. Meagher and his Irish Brigade amid the narrow valley of the Rappahannock River. In terms of tenacity and fighting spirit, the Twenty-fourth Georgia proved to be a worthy match for the Irish Brigade on December 12, 1862. One British observer reflected upon the scene at Fredericksburg: "Southern Irishmen make excellent 'Rebs,' and have no sort of scruple in killing as many of their northern brethren as they possibly can."

A tough, reliable command organized in the summer of 1861, the Twenty-fourth Georgia was heavily Irish. Its members hailed from Irish enclaves in large cities, small towns, and rural areas across Georgia. The story of the Twenty-fourth Georgia provides good evidence of the extent of the ethnic clannishness of the Confederate Irish not only in terms of community, but also of family.

Col. Robert Emmet McMillan, Sr., born in County Antrim, Ireland, on January 7, 1805, commanded the Twenty-fourth Georgia. His first and middle names, honoring the Irish rebel and patriot Robert Emmet, bestowed an inspirational revolutionary example at an early age. After departing his homeland, McMillan thrived in America. He became a leading citizen of the Savannah River country in Elbert County, Georgia, and was elected to the Georgia state legislature. The transplanted Irishman married in 1833, and his first son, Robert Emmet McMillan, Jr., was born in 1835. As so often was the case with the Confederate Irish, the name of Robert Emmet invoked a distinguished revolutionary heritage from the Emerald Isle that was alive and well in America. In addition, this influence also transcended generational lines, looming as a reminder of the high cost of freedom. This identical revolutionary influence was also reflected on the Union side. Ireland-born Gen. Robert Emmet Patterson, Sr., was proud of the fact that his son, Col. Robert Emmet Patterson, Jr., was a West Pointer in command of the One hundred-and-fifteenth Pennsylvania Volunteer Infantry. This regiment contained many Irishmen from Philadelphia and across Pennsylvania.

During the Civil War, Colonel McMillan's son served as the major of the Twenty-fourth Georgia. The clannish and familial qualities of the Confederate Irish experience was especially evident with Colonel McMillan commanding the Twenty-fourth Georgia Regiment, while his eldest son, Major McMillan, was third in command. In addition, Capt. Garnett McMillan, a younger son, led an Irish company in the same regiment. Clearly, the McMillan clan of Georgia Confederates included not only a capable father-son leadership team but also a brother team of officers as well.

The defining moment of the Irish Brigade, Army of the Potomac, was its doomed, frontal attack on the stone wall at Fredericksburg on December 13, 1862. The dramatic assault of the Irish Brigade on this "Bloody Sunday" was a display of heroism that became legendary across the North. While the Irish Brigade won fame for its role in the battle of Fredericksburg, the task of the Confederate Irish of the Twenty-fourth Georgia who

Marye's House in Fredericksburg, Maryland, close to where the Twenty-fourth Georgia fought the Irish Brigade.

defended the stone wall against their fellow Irishmen in blue has been largely forgotten.

The sight of the attack of the Irishmen in blue was awe-inspiring. More than 1,300 Irish Yankees surged forward with firm discipline, while the green flags of Ireland proudly waved over the surging blue ranks under a pale winter sky. The lengthy assault formations of the Irish Brigade rolled forward like clock-work, moving with a precision that brought a sense of admiration to both friend and foe. Hundreds of the bluecoat Irishmen poured across the grim killing fields of Fredericksburg to uphold the honor of their adopted homeland, their regiments, and old Ireland. Gen. Thomas F. Meagher's soldiers continued toward the fortified high ground of Marye's Heights with not only green battle-flags flapping in the cold December air but also with green sprigs of boxwood in their blue kepis. This garnishment represented pride in their distinctive ethnicity and honored their native homeland. The Irish Brigade's assault was one of the grand spectacles of the war, though one of the most suicidal as well because thousands of veterans of the Army of Northern Virginia were waiting in excellent defensive positions on high ground.

At the foot of Marye's Heights stood the stone wall and a little sunken road, crammed full of seasoned Confederate infantry. Atop Marye's Heights, rows of southern cannon reflected the weak sunlight of early winter. Among the Confederate artillery pieces turned upon the onrushing Irish Brigade was the famous Washington Artillery from New Orleans. This unit included a good many Irish cannoneers such as privates P. Leahy, a teenage painter, J.L. Matthews, and J. McCormack.

Colonel McMillan and the soldiers of the Twenty-fourth Georgia, under the overall command of Gen. Thomas Reade Rootes Cobb, were poised behind the stone wall at the foot of Marye's Heights while the onrushing Irish Brigade moved ever closer. To the Twenty-fourth Georgia's right stood the gray ranks of the Eighteenth Georgia Infantry. The Eighteenth

Georgia waited in position behind the wall of stone, while Phillips' Legion of Georgia troops were aligned behind the stone wall to Colònel McMillan's left. These reliable veterans of Cobb's brigade bolstered the confidence of the Twenty-fourth Georgia defenders as they faced the onslaught of the Irish Brigade and several thousand other Federal soldiers.

Thomas R.R. Cobb was a lawyer and politician in Georgia before becoming commander of the Twenty-fourth Georgia during the Battle of Fredericksburg where he was killed while fighting the Irish Brigade.

The Confederate soldiers remained quiet in their firing positions, with smoothbore and rifled muskets trained on the Irish Brigade. The majority of the weapons of the Twenty-fourth Georgia defenders were the reliable smoothbore musket loaded with "buck and ball." The gun held a large caliber lead ball and three buckshot, making the firearm a most effective shotgun, especially deadly at close range. Such a killing tool was guaranteed to wreak havoc upon the neat, tidy ranks of the onrushing Irish Brigade. Colonel McMillan realized as much and formulated his tactics to maximize the effectiveness of his regiment's weaponry. He planned to allow the charging Irishmen to get as close as possible to the stone wall before ordering the Twenty-fourth Georgia to open fire.

Consequently, Georgia defenders possessed plenty of time to view the sweeping attack of the Irish Brigade, which poured over the rolling plain that led to Marye's Heights. Meanwhile, the Irish Brigade's "deep rich green" battle-flags emblazoned with the gold harps of Ireland and adorned with the slogan "They shall never retreat from the charge of lances," came ever-closer to the stone wall. Nevertheless, the Confederate soldiers resisted the temptation of opening fire before ordered, though they found the task increasingly difficult.

Colonel McMillan's reliance on firm discipline at this critical moment now paid dividends. Some Irish Rebels of the Twenty-fourth Georgia may have expressed a measure of disgust in what was often said when Lee's men caught sight of the green banners of the Irish Brigade, "Here comes that damned green flag again!" Colonel McMillan's Irish troops may have felt not only respect for their fellow countrymen in blue, but also a sense of tragedy for the cruel events about to unfold.

Sensing his troops' anxiety, Colonel McMillan took action to guarantee that no premature shots were fired, shouting "Hold. Don't fire yet. Wait till I give the order." All the while, hundreds of Irish Brigade veterans continued to rush forward across the open fields with discipline and almost perfect alignment. The sight was impressive, but Colonel McMillan repeated his order, drawing the Irish Brigade closer to the Confederate guns. The Federal infantrymen were so close to the stone wall that it appeared as if the assault would steamroll over the Confederate defenders.

Colonel McMillan maintained his nerve in the face of the blue onslaught until the Federals reached approximately 50 yards from the stone wall. An anxious Twenty-fourth Georgia soldier finally broke the tense silence by shouting to the commander: "Colonel, we must fire, they are coming too close!" McMillan gave no immediate reply, but shortly thereafter gave the order to fire shouting "men, if you do shoot, shoot low."

The entire 600-yard length of the stone wall at the foot of Marye's Heights exploded with fire when all the Georgians pulled their triggers in unison. A sheet of flame erupted in the faces of the attacking Irish Brigade troops, dropping scores of soldiers like ten pins. The cherished green battle-flags went down as well, but were quickly raised by surviving members of the Irish Brigade's regimental color guard. Pvt. William McCarter of the One Hundred and Sixteenth Pennsylvania never forgot the terrible moment "when a large part of the distance had been gained and we were within 50 paces of this wall, Cobb's solid brigade of Rebel infantry, said to have been then 2,400 strong, suddenly sprang up from behind it [as] they had been entirely concealed from our view until that moment. The Rebs poured volley after volley into our faces . . ."

Near the crest of Marye's Heights above and to the right of the blazing stone wall, one young cannoneer of the Washington Artillery, William M. Owen, described the horror of the scene below: "bearing aloft the green flag with the golden harp of Ireland those brave fellows came within five-and-twenty paces of the stone-wall and encountered such a fire of shot, shell, canister, and musketry as no command was ever known to live through." The Irish Brigade suffered tremendously in their assault on the stone wall. Hundreds of Irishmen in blue fell to the scorching fires from both artillery and musketry.

Lee also felt a sense of admiration for the heroic perform-ance of the Irish Brigade soldiers, who continued to charge straight into the flaming wall of stone. Upon witnessing the decimation of the Irish Brigade Lee declared, "never were men so brave." As if coming to the same conclusion, one Irish Rebel of the Twenty-fourth Georgia suddenly raised his hat into the smoke-laced air and gave a cheer to the Irish Brigade soldiers. More Georgia Rebels took off and waved their slouch hats and gray kepis to acknowledge the bravery of the Irish Brigade. Perhaps some fallen Irish Brigade soldiers nearest the stone wall heard the rising tide of Confederate cheering from the stone wall, but they probably assumed that the eruption of noise indicated the attack's repulse, not realizing it to actually be a rare tribute to the fallen Union soldiers.

Pvt. James Williams, "a mere boy," was so overcome with emotion at the sight of the Irish Brigade's charge that he leaped "upon the top of the [stone] wall and gave three ringing cheers, waving his hat, before his comrades could pull him down," recalled Pvt. E.H. Sutton, of the Twenty-fourth Georgia. Sutton described Colonel McMillan's inspirational leadership during the assault: "Colonel Robert McMillan was passing up and down the line all the time exposing himself, but making the boys keep down behind the [stone] wall [and] at last a spent ball struck him about the neck. His son, Garnett, saw it and called out, 'Pa, are you hurt?' 'Hit, but not hurt' came the answer, and stooping down he picked up the ball and placed it in his vest pocket." Capt. Garnett McMillan then grabbed a rifled musket and concentrated his efforts on killing Union sharpshooters.

The Confederate soldiers successfully defended the stone wall at Fredericksburg and the Irish Brigade received devastating losses of more than 500 men. Thanks in part to the hard-fighting Twenty-fourth Georgia at Fredericksburg, Lee and the Army of Northern Virginia won another impressive victory. Fredericksburg was a disastrous loss for the Army of the Potomac. As on other battlefields across the South, the Irish in America once again waged their own civil war against each other at the small town of Fredericksburg.

At Lee's surrender at Appomattox Courthouse on Palm Sunday 1865, only a handful of soldiers from the Twenty-fourth Georgia remained to lay down their arms. Among those Irishmen left standing at the war's end were Surgeon L.D. McMannen, Sgt. D. McCurdy, Pvt. W.J. Morgan, Pvt. G. McGarrity, and Pvt. William Henry Wade.

CHAPTER 4

Irishmen of the First Missouri Confederate Brigade at the Battle of Champion Hill, Mississippi, May 16, 1863

The impressive combat record of the First Missouri Confederate Brigade equaled the sterling combat record of the more famous Stonewall, Orphan, and Iron brigades. While its reputation is not well known today, it was widely recognized during the war years by people across the Confederacy. One Mississippi officer described in an early 1864 letter how the elite troops of the Missouri Brigade were "the brag of this or any other army, they fight better, drill better, and look better than any other men in the army."

A variety of factors explain why the hard-fighting soldiers of the First Missouri Confederate Brigade were among the best and most reliable combat troops throughout the war. Many Irish officers and enlisted men had served in various militia regiments before the start of the conflict, or had gained some military experience in the Mexican-American War. With a tinge of humor, Lt. Joseph Boyce, whose parents were Ireland-born, described the First and Fourth Missouri Confederate Infantry (Consolidated) Regiment, as "this Irish crowd." By the time of the Battle of Champion Hill in mid-May 1863, the third-highest-ranking officer of the unit was Ireland-born Maj. Martin Burke, who had served in the St. Louis Greys, an antebellum militia company. Most of all, these Irish Confederates from St. Louis and the outlying rural counties of Missouri were considered to have been the best, most reliable, and hardest fighting soldiers of the First Missouri Brigade.

Most Irish of the First Missouri Brigade served in the ranks of the First and Fourth Missouri (Consolidated) Regiment or the Third and Fifth Missouri (Consolidated) Regiment, though Irishmen served in other units as well. Before the war, Irishmen dominated the militia ranks of the Washington Blues, the Montgomery Guards, and the Emmet Guards. The men of these militia companies were considered to be the best drilled soldiers of Missouri's antebellum militias, a legacy continued by the Emerald Islanders in Confederate service.

Many young Celts hailed from the Irish community on St. Louis's north side known as Kerry Patch, named for County Kerry in southwest Ireland. Service in the prestigious militia of St. Louis provided social mobility for these Irishmen, who festooned themselves in distinctive shamrock-decorated breastplates that adorned their blue militia uniforms. They also sang patriotic Irish tunes, including revolutionary ballads from the 1798 and 1848 Irish uprisings against the British. The revolutionary traditions of Ireland thrived in St. Louis in the decades before the Civil War. The silk battle-flag of the Emmet Guards was distinguished by a portrait of George Washington on one side and Robert Emmet on the other, with Emmet's revolutionary slogan spoken just before his execution: "I have wished to procure for my country the guarantee which Washington procured for America."

Most of all, the Irishmen from the Mississippi River port city wanted to even the score with the hated German "Hessians" of St. Louis. "Hessian" was the name Irishmen used for the British soldiers who occupied the Green Isle and the German soldiers hired as mercenaries by King George III during the American Revolution. Anti-Catholic and anti-Irish riots in St. Louis during the 1850s helped to heighten the Irish hatred toward the Germans and even the United States. Many St. Louis Irish discovered to their dismay that the hypocrisy and discrimination of the New World were not so different from that of the Old World. The idea of a vibrant new southern nation born in the revolutionary experience might provide a better life for the Irish people. Therefore, when Confederate guns opened fire on Fort Sumter in April 1861, the St. Louis Irish were driven into "a state of frenzy," flocking to the defense of both the state and the South.

Many Irish soldiers from St. Louis, such as Missouri Brigade officers Patrick Canniff and Martin Burke, brought with them years of valuable military experience with the companies of the Missouri Volunteer Militia. Because of their previous militia experiences the Irish soldiers of the Missouri Brigade were noted far and wide for their proficiency at drill and discipline. One Confederate soldier from St. Louis asserted how Company F of the Fifth Missouri was "without doubt one of the best companies in the Confederate army [because] it was drilled to perfection [and] it was the pride of the Missouri division." A Missouri Confederate from the Missouri River country wrote how he briefly marched beside "a company [F] of Irishmen from St. Louis—all Irish from the captain [Patrick Canniff] down. They were recruited [from] the wharves of St. Louis. Brave men and good soldiers they proved themselves to be . . . how proud I would be to have been on the roll of this company."

As in other southern units, the Confederate Irish of the Missouri Brigade were often employed in the most demanding battlefield roles: spearheading attacks, skirmish duty before the front lines, and protecting the brigade's rear during risky withdrawals. While fighting on battlefields in Missouri, Arkansas, Mississippi, Tennessee, Louisiana, Georgia, and Alabama from 1861-1865, the Missouri Brigade mastered these critical roles. The casualty rates of the Irishmen in Company F, the all-Irish company of the Fifth Missouri, attested to the frequent use of veteran soldiers for such dangerous tasks. Among these hard-fighting soldiers, primarily from St. Louis, were: Sgt. John Brennan, age twenty-two; Pvt. John Chambers, a thirty-year-old stone cutter; Pvt. Joseph Glassford, age twenty-seven; Sgt. Thomas Hogan, a twenty-two-year-old clerk; Pvt. William Mallony, a twenty-year-old saddler; a clerk named Pvt. Patrick McGrath, age twenty-six; Pvt. Daniel Monahan; Pvt. Peter Moran, age thirty-seven from Morgan County, Missouri; and Sgt. William Walsh, a twenty-eight-year-old merchant and color bearer of the regiment. All of these Ireland-born soldiers were killed in the war.

In addition, other companies of the Missouri Brigade were sprinkled with Irishmen. Company H, Fifth Missouri, contained several Irish soldiers including: Pvt. John Cunningham, age thirty-two and a peddler; Pvt. Patrick Burke, a thirty-year-old laborer; and Cpl. Edward Fitzgerald, a twenty-seven-year-old laborer from Warrensburg, Missouri.

The unshakable humor of the Missouri Brigade Irish became legendary throughout the western armies. Capt. Samuel T. Foster, of Gen. Hiram Granbury's Texas Brigade, Army of Tennessee, recorded in his reminiscences a memorable visit by the former governor of Texas, Col. Francis Richard Lubbock, who served on President Jefferson Davis's personal staff in 1864 at the time when the Confederate president visited the Army of Tennessee. During the last week of September 1864, Colonel Lubbock visited the Texas soldiers of Gen. Matthew Duncan Ector's largely Lone Star State brigade of Gen. Samuel French's Division, which included the First Missouri Brigade. In Captain Foster's words: "now it so happened that F.R. Lubbock late Governor of Texas was on Davis' staff, and he naturally supposing that the Texas soldiers would be glad to see him, thought he would take this occasion to introduce himself and we would give him a grand cheer—He made a serious mistake and so spoiled the whole thing. He stoped [sic] in front of an Irish Regt. [the First and Fourth Missouri (Consolidated)] just on our right before he got to us. Thinking he had found us, rode square up about the centre pulled off his hat and says 'I am Governor Lubbock of Texas' and just when he expected to hear a big cheer, an Irishman says 'An' who the bloody Hell is govener [*sic*] Lubbock?' with that peculiar Irish brogue, that made the Governor wilt."

By the time of the Vicksburg campaign, the Irish soldiers of the Missouri Brigade possessed a widespread reputation not only for ferocity in combat but also for proficiency at drill. These two characteristics would soon be tested during a critical tactical situation at the Battle of Champion Hill, Mississippi, on May 16, 1863.

Gen. John C. Pemberton—saddled with the responsibility of protecting Vicksburg without sufficient support and with too few troops—was caught unprepared for battle when the advance elements of Gen. Ulysses S. Grant's army pushed rapidly westward from the state capital of Jackson, Mississippi, toward Vicksburg, the vital bastion on the Mississippi River. If possession of Vicksburg and the Mississippi River be could retained by the Confederacy, then the southern nation might well survive its infancy. Responding to threats from the Federal advance, Pemberton hurriedly realigned his army eastward to face the ever-aggressive Grant.

Unknown to Pemberton, Grant's forces moved toward Vicksburg in multiple columns. Federal troops aligned themselves in advantageous positions both in front of Gen. Pemberton's army and on the left flank. Occupying Pemberton's center was Gen. John Stevens Bowen's Division, which contained the Missouri Brigade. To slow the enemy's advance and to protect the Missouri Brigade's front, five companies of skirmishers, along with other units, pushed eastward. Two of these companies were under the command of Ireland-born officers, captains Patrick Canniff and Martin Burke, both from St. Louis.

Meanwhile, a full Union division attacked from the northeast and perpendicular to the hastily-formed Confederate battle line which now faced east. These Federals tore savagely into Pemberton's exposed left flank, smashing the foremost Rebel units and gaining ground. In short order and by the early afternoon of May 16, a full Confederate division was destroyed by the rising blue tide, and Pemberton's left disintegrated under the onslaught. Next in line to face the Union attack was Bowen's Division in the center, which seemed likely to suffer the same dismal fate.

To meet the enemy's advance, Bowen turned his division north and rushed his two brigades forward in a desperate effort to stem the flow of oncoming Federals. Before the attack, Bowen attempted to form his two brigades in a battle line, but on the left, the Missouri Brigade struggled to comply with the general's order. It was critical to Bowen's counterattack that the Missouri Brigade's battle line be complete before the Union attack could be reversed. The crisis was greatest on the Missouri Brigade's right, where the First and Fourth Missouri (Consolidated) was located. Reliable Irishmen served in this regiment, including Pvt. John Dempsey, who was fated to be killed during the Georgia campaign of 1864; Sgt. Thomas H. Murphy, a thirty-three-year-old boatman from St. Louis; and Lt. John Redmond of St. Louis. During the battle Ireland-born Father John B. Bannon of St. Louis passed down the battle line of gray, giving communion to as many soldiers as possible.

Heavy pressure from the attacking Federal troops forced the Missourians to fall back a short distance, causing other Confederate regiments on the left to likewise give ground because of the vicious flank fire. The situation became more precarious as the battle continued because not only the Missouri Brigade, but also Bowen's entire division, was in danger. Despite the desperate circumstances, the Confederates finally aligned themselves and unleashed several point-blank volleys into the bluecoat attackers, allowing the First and Fourth Missouri (Consolidated) to surge forward into the midst of the oncoming Federal charge. The hard-hitting Confederates regained lost ground and stabilized the brigade line by anchoring the right flank of the Missouri Brigade. Along with the never-say-die attitude of the many Irish soldiers in the ranks, officers such as Captain Burke, and regimental commander Col. Amos Camden Riley (later killed during the 1864 Atlanta campaign), played key roles in the Confederate movement to regain position and control of the battle front.

By the early afternoon, the 2,000-man Missouri Brigade was finally ready to launch a counterattack to save Pemberton's army from destruction. The Confederate army needed every available soldier (even sick men and boys) to reverse the momentum of battle. Pvt. Thomas Doyle from St. Louis was a twenty-two-year-old Ireland-born baker who had already lost an arm in battle. Nevertheless he rejoined the fray in the ranks of the Fifth Missouri, now commanded by a tough Irish-American, Col. James McCown.

With flags flying and the rebel yell erupting from their mouths, the Missouri Confederates advanced, driving the bluecoats back, recapturing lost batteries, and gaining much ground. Bitter hand-to-hand fighting swirled over the rough terrain among the magnolias, deep gullies, and dense woodlands of Champion Hill. One man from the First and Fourth Missouri (Consolidated), Pvt. David M. Gill, carried the regimental colors and led his fellow soldiers forward into the tempest, all the while ignoring a serious wound. Federal troops, including the brigade commanded by a hard-fighting Irish-American general named George Francis McGinnis, were hurled rearward by the slashing Missouri counterattack.

Attacking on the brigade's right while exposed to flank fire, the First and Fourth Missouri (Consolidated) suffered severely. Among the Irishmen of Colonel Riley's regiment who would not survive the day was "Wild Pat" Doolen, a twenty-five-year-old laborer from St. Louis. Some of the finest officers of the Fifth Missouri were killed during the bitter contest in the bloody woodlands, including Irishman Capt. Harvey G. McKinney, who led the soldiers of Company H.

Vicious fighting continued through the forests of Champion Hill. An inspiring influence to the Irish troops was the spirited performance of Pvt. Daniel Monahan of Company F, Fifth Missouri. Monahan led the company forward through the smoke-filled forest, and then fought hand-to-hand with the stubborn Federals. In the words of an amazed Lt. Col. Robert S. Bevier, Private Monahan, using his Enfield rifled musket as a club, "commenced striking right and left, with mad energy, while a thousand bullets, from both sides, whistled around him [and] his long hair streaming in the wind, the Herculean blows he made, and the [curses] with which he accompanied each one, gave him the appearance of being some avenging" Celtic angel of death. Private Monahan was mortally wounded during the Atlanta campaign of 1864.

Besides the First and Fourth Missouri (Consolidated) and the Fifth Missouri, a rural regiment primarily from the Missouri River country also containing many Irish, the Third Missouri, which was attached to the Fifth Missouri's left. All of these regiments advanced forward as one. The Third Missouri included a good many reliable Ireland-born soldiers: Cpl. Richard Burke from Liberty, later mortally wounded during the Georgia campaign; Lt. James T. Carby, a twenty-two-year-old merchant from the Missouri River port of St. Joseph; Sgt. Maj. John Carroll, a stone mason from Plattsburg; thirty-nine-year-old Cpl. Michael Flood from Albany; Pvt. Matthew Madegan, a teenager from St. Joseph; a twenty-nine-year-old brick layer named Charles McDennis; and Pvt. Michael O'Brien, a farmer from Liberty, to name a few.

Bowen's assault was on the verge of splitting Grant's army in two when at the last minute a massed array of Union cannon and large numbers of reinforcements thwarted the sweeping counterattack of Bowen's Division, depriving the Confederates of success. Halted by the lengthy blue formations and booming cannon, the Missourians in gray gamely maintained their advanced positions, returning fire with spirit. Bowen's men now hoped in vain for the arrival of Confederate reinforcements. The two brigades of Bowen's Division suffered high casualties during the assault, and soldiers began to run low on ammunition.

Nevertheless, the Missouri Brigade continued to hold firm under heavy fire and the mounting pressure of reinforced Federal units. When a number of artillerymen were cut down while working the cannon of two Missouri batteries that provided protective fire for the Missouri Brigade, Father Bannon joined the action as a member of a gun crew of Capt. Henry Guibor's Missouri Battery. During the nightmarish fighting at Champion Hill, Father Bannon worked in unison with the surviving artillerymen, adding to his reputation as "the Fighting Chaplain" from Ireland.

This was an ethnic artillary unit which contained a large percentage of Irishmen from the docks and wharves of St. Louis. Captain Guibor's unit was now under the able command of Ireland-born Lt. William Corkery, age twenty-seven, of St. Louis. By this time, Captain Guibor's Battery played a vital role in protecting what little was left of the Missouri infantry, low on ammunition and manpower. The roaring guns of Captain Guibor's Battery now anchored the Missouri Brigade's vulnerable left flank, which remained under heavy pressure. The rapid fire of these Missouri artillery pieces helped keep the advancing blue formations at bay. Among the Irish cannoneers of Guibor's Battery was Lieutenant Corkery's second in command, Ireland-born Lt. Cornelius Heffernan, age twenty-five and a clerk from St. Louis.

Meanwhile, Capt. William Wade's Battery anchored the Missouri Brigade's right flank. Like Captain Guibor's Battery, Captain Wade's Battery contained many St. Louis Irish in the ranks: twenty-eight-year-old Lt. James Barron; Pvt. William Brooks, age fifty-three; twenty-one-year-old Pvt. Maurice Daniels; Pvt. James Kane, age twenty-nine; Lt. John Kearney, age thirty-three; and twenty-six-year-old Lt. Richard C. Walsh.

Grant's fierce counterattack, bolstered by thousands of additional reinforcements, ultimately decided the fate of the battle. Bowen's Division retired from the field, leaving hundreds of its men, including a good many Irishmen, in the bloody woodlands of Hinds County, Mississippi. With the Confederate defeat at Champion Hill, the stage was set for the final demise of Vicksburg. Pemberton's beaten army withdrew west into the fortifications of the Mississippi River port city. Grant invested the city in a siege which lasted forty-seven agonizing days. The end for Vicksburg came on the Fourth of July 1863. Vicksburg's capture was a decisive Union success that sealed the fate of both the Mississippi River and the Confederacy as well. With the fall of Vicksburg, the Confederacy received a death stroke from which it would never recover.

CHAPTER 5

The Irish Rebels of the Fifteenth Alabama Infantry Storm Little Round Top, July 2, 1863

Col. Joshua Lawrence Chamberlain's own prolific writings, John Pullen's 1957 book entitled *The Twentieth Maine*, Michael Shaara's 1974 Pulitzer Prize-winning novel *Killer Angels*, and the 1994 film "Gettysburg" all immortalized the struggle for possession of Little Round Top at Gettysburg, Colonel Chamberlain, and his Twentieth Maine Volunteer Infantry. So much publicity and recognition has been garnered by Colonel Chamberlain and the Twentieth Maine that a romantic mythology has risen up to popularize both the Maine regiment and its commander to an extent not seen even during the Civil War Centennial.

While the role of the Twentieth Maine during the small unit action of Little Round Top against the Fifteenth Alabama Infantry has been analyzed extensively, the role of Col. William C. Oates's

Fifteenth Alabama has been largely unrecognized and over-looked. One of the most forgotten features of the struggle for pos-session of Little Round Top on the bloody afternoon of July 2, 1863, was the role of the Confederate Irish who fought in the Fifteenth Alabama.

Company K was the most ethnically distinct company of the Fifteenth Alabama. In Colonel Oates's words, ". . . it was an Irish company." He also described how "a large

Joshua Lawrence Chamberlain was the com-mander of the Twentieth Maine during the assault on Little Round Top.

percentage of this company [K] were Irish laborers," many of whom were recent immi-grants while only a few were second genera-tion Irish Americans. Colonel Oates was pleased with his ethnic company not only because of its fighting prowess and high state of discipline but also due to considerable pride in his own Irish heritage.

Some of Company K's Irish soldiers had reached America by landing at Pensacola, Florida. From the major gulf ports of Mobile and Pensacola, the Irish had migrated north up the Tombigbee and Chattahoochee Rivers. Drawn by economic opportunity and the dream of a new life in America, the Irish settled in south-east Alabama river towns along the Chattahoochee River like Eufaula, Alabama. Other immigrants continued to migrate far-ther up river, settling at Columbus, Georgia, on the eastern border of Alabama. The Chattahoochee River served as a point of entry into the Alabama interior for many immigrant Irish.

With the call to arms in April 1861, some ninety Irishmen enlisted in Company K, Fifteenth Alabama, at Eufaula in

Barbour County, Alabama. In fact, most Company K Irish hailed from Barbour County, though Irishmen from Henry and Dale counties, located farther down the Chattahoochee River, were represented in the company as well. Most Fifteenth Alabama Irishmen were common laborers. Colonel Oates described them as "generally belong[ing] to the floating population of the country," from the busy river traffic and ports along the Chattahoochee.

During the Pennsylvania invasion, Lt. William J. Bethune, one of the original company officers, led the spunky Irish Rebels of Company K. Past company commanders experienced so much trouble in controlling the unruly spirits of the Irishmen in Company K that they resigned in frustration. This was not the case of Lieutenant Bethune. He was as tough as the Irishmen he commanded, and earned respect, if not popularity, in the process. If his Irishmen disobeyed an order or offered defiance to his authority, Lieutenant Bethune would simply resort to his fists to control his troublesome soldiers.

Both on and off the battlefield, Lieutenant Bethune depended heavily upon reliable non-commissioned officers, such as twenty-six-year-old Sgt. James H. Gray. He was "a fine soldier" in Colonel Oates's estimation. Sergeant Gray would rise to the challenge of Gettysburg and future campaigns across Virginia. He was destined to earn an officer's rank and an early grave in the South before the conclusion of 1863.

One typical Irish lad of Company K, Fifteenth Alabama, was a plucky young musician named Patrick F. Brannon. At age thirteen, the musically-inclined Rebel was the youngest member of the company, and one of the youngest drummer boys of the Fifteenth Alabama. He was a second generation Irishman. His Catholic parents were among the Potato Famine Irish who fled the Emerald Isle in the mid-1840s. Pat's older brother, Pvt. Thomas Brannon, also of Company K, was killed at Second Manassas at the end of August 1862. His brother's death in Virginia came as a severe blow to the young man, leaving Patrick "an orphan . . . without a home . . ."

Pat Brannon was one of the favorites of not only Company K but also of the entire Fifteenth Alabama. He was well-known for his endless pranks and mischievous nature, which made him an unending source of both popularity and irritation. Colonel Oates developed much affection for the "orphan." Oates described Brannon as "a very intelligent, manly boy [who] was never sick, always at his post, and a great favorite of the men [and] he became well versed in the arts of gambling. He had one trick called 'the string game,' and by it he won large sums of Confederate money from the soldiers. I saw that he was becoming too much infatuated with gambling and feared that it would ruin him, and ordered him to quit it and not engage in it any more." Colonel Oates's fatherly influence paid spiritual dividends, as the young drummer boy became a respected Catholic priest after the war.

While drummer boy Pat Brannon was one of Company K's most popular members, Sgt. Patrick O'Connor was the heart and soul of the Irish group. In fact, the twenty-three-year-old Ireland-born soldier was one of the most inspirational influences in the entire regiment. All ranks of the regiment considered Sergeant O'Connor to be the hardest fighting and toughest non-commissioned officer of the Fifteenth Alabama. Most important, Colonel Oates could depend more on Sergeant O'Connor than any other non-commissioned officer of his elite regiment.

Before his enlistment in Company K at Eufaula, O'Connor labored as a tinner. Colonel Oates described O'Connor as being " . . . more intelligent than any of the other" member of Company K. This hardy Irishman first enlisted as a private but quickly rose through the ranks as his leadership ability and bravery became evident on the battlefield. Like so many Fifteenth Alabama Irish, the incomparable Sergeant O'Connor was fated to receive his death stroke from Yankee bullets during the late spring of 1864.

The decisive showdown at Gettysburg took shape under the hot summer sun. Lee and the Army of Northern Virginia successfully drove the Federals from the western outskirts of Gettysburg and through the town on July 1. Union troops took good defensive positions on the high ground of Cemetery Ridge and awaited the Rebels' next move on the morning of July 2.

Refusing to forsake the initiative and determined to exploit the gains of the first day's battle, Lee decided to continue the offensive on July 2. He ordered Gen. James Longstreet and the entire First Corps to extend the army's battle line southward in order to strike at the Union army's left flank. Young Gen. Evander McIver Law, of Gen. John Bell Hood's division, formed his brigade of Alabama Rebels, including the Fifteenth Alabama, on the far right flank of Lee's army. Colonel Oates and his regiment, including the Irishmen of Company K, aligned in the Alabama brigade's center. After a lengthy delay

A photograph of the breastworks at Little Round Top with Big Round Top in the background.

and in the heat of early afternoon on July 2, the Alabamians moved forward with battle-flags flying, initiating the assault by not only Law's troops, but also the remainder of Longstreet's First Corps.

At the advance's beginning, the Fifteenth Alabama surged past the six booming guns of the First North Carolina Artillery. This battery was under the command of Ireland-born Capt. James Reilly, who Colonel Oates described as "a burly old Irishman." The hard-fighting Captain Reilly, born in Athlone, County Westmeath located in the central plains of Ireland, was nicknamed the "Old Tarantula," because he was "rough, gruff, grizzly, and brave." He was an artillery veteran of the Mexican and Seminole Wars. Captain Reilly ended his military career in a Federal prison after he was captured during the fall of Fort Fisher, North Carolina, in early 1865.

Law ordered a realignment of his forces and Colonel Oates's Fifteenth Alabama moved to anchor the brigade's right flank. The troops progressed as the southernmost Rebels on Lee's extreme right flank. The advancing Confederates fell under heavy fire from Col. Hiram Berdan's Sharpshooters. These Union marksmen made a defiant stand, blasting away with their repeating rifles behind a stone wall at the western base of Big Round Top, which stood adjacent to and just south of Little Round Top.

Colonel Oates continued to lead his soldiers onward through the brisk rifle fire, pushing the Federal marksmen rearward and up the steep slope of Big Round Top. A running fight between the Alabama Rebels and the crack Union marksmen ensued over fallen trees, rocks, and huge boulders that covered the steep slope of the highest mountain in Adams County, Pennsylvania. After more hard fighting and a straight advance eastward, the Fifteenth Alabama finally gained the imposing, rock-crowned summit of Big Round Top. After a brief rest, the Alabamians swarmed down the thickly forested hill and advanced north and up the adjacent hill, Little Round Top. In good defensive positions on high ground, the Twentieth Maine, along with the remainder of Col. Strong Vincent's veteran brigade, awaited the Rebel assault.

After an unexpected close-range volley, Colonel Oates ordered his Alabamians to charge up the slope. Leading the Irish Rebels of Company K, Lieutenant Bethune, who was "not very popular among his men on account of the rigidity of his discipline," fell when struck in the face by a minie ball. Despite the death of their company commander, the Irish Confederates of Company K continued to attack up the slope with flashing bayonets and Celtic war cries.

Not all of the Irish performed with courage or spirit at Little Round Top, however. Pvt. John Nelson, age twenty-three, had grown weary of facing veteran Yankees, who had become as tenacious fighters as the Johnny Rebs. Bethune, therefore, ordered Sergeant O'Connor "to hold Nelson to his work." When the fire pouring downhill from the Maine muskets became too much for the young man, Private Nelson attempted to bolt rearward to escape. Colonel Oates, who had no sympathy for cowardice on the battlefield, recalled: "O'Conner [sic] collared him and held him to his place until he was killed. O'Conner [sic] was also an Irishman, and one of the bravest. Nelson died trying to flee instead of bravely facing the foe. As O'Conner [sic] let him down he said, 'Now I guess you will not run away.'"

Besides the unfortunate Private Nelson, other Irish soldiers of Company K fell in their desperate attempts to hurl Colonel Chamberlain's Maine regiment off the high ground of Little Round Top. Irishmen killed in the assault included twenty-one-year-old Pvt. James M. Brown; Pvt. William T. Bynum, age eighteen; and Pvt. James Rutledge, age thirty-four. No matter how many times Colonel Oates hurled his Alabama attackers up the timbered slope of Little Round Top, they were greeted by an eruption of musketry from the Springfield rifles of the Twentieth Maine soldiers. Nevertheless, the Rebels continued to launch one assault after another, hoping to drive the stubborn bluecoats from their high ground perch.

Savage hand-to-hand combat erupted when the blue and gray lines repeatedly clashed on the smoke-laced spur of Little Round Top. In yet another desperate attack uphill, Colonel Oates and Sergeant O'Connor encouraged their Rebels forward into the cauldron of blazing musketry, while the regimental color bearer carried the flag nearby and led the way for all to see. Sergeant O'Connor served as an inspirational example for not only the Irish of Company K but also the entire regiment. When a Maine soldier attempted to wrestle the colors from the Alabama flag bearer, Colonel Oates recalled that Sergeant O'Connor "stove his bayonet through the head of the Yankee, who fell dead."

Despite the high sacrifice, the relentless efforts of Colonel Oates and his Fifteenth Alabama were in vain. High casualties, no reinforcements, and lack of ammunition guaranteed that the assault to capture Little Round Top and turn the Army of the Potomac's left flank was doomed to failure. Exploiting the situation, troops from the Twentieth Maine advanced down the body-littered slope of Little Round Top and drove the last Alabama soldiers rearward, securing the far southern, or left, flank of the Union army.

Gettysburg was a turning point of the war, leading the southern nation farther down the road to extinction. Confederate failure to capture Little Round Top on July 2, the day before "Pickett's Charge" on Cemetery Ridge, all but ensured that Lee and the Army of Northern Virginia would suffer a decisive defeat in south-central Pennsylvania in early July 1863. As throughout the war, more young men in gray and butternut from the Emerald Isle had died in vain for a dream that would never come true.

CHAPTER 6

Irish and Southern Nationalism Merge During "Pickett's Charge" and at the "High Water Mark of the Confederacy," July 3, 1863

On the sweltering afternoon of July 3, 1863, Gen. Robert E. Lee decided to launch a desperate bid to win the Battle of Gettysburg by unleashing "Pickett's Charge" against the formidable Union positions along Cemetery Ridge. Because of Confederate failure to reap decisive success the previous day, Lee ordered "Pickett's Charge" in an attempt to split the Army of the Potomac and open up the road for the Army of Northern Virginia to threaten major northern cities.

In the annals of Civil War historiography, this futile attempt of Lee to win decisive victory on the third day of Gettysburg has been viewed as one of Virginia's finest days.

The bloody offensive effort known as "Pickett's Charge" has often been identified as largely a Virginia effort at the expense of thousands of other attackers, especially the North Carolina troops who charged forward with Gen. George E. Pickett's Division of Virginians. The efforts of the many Irish Confederates from both Virginia and North Carolina who rushed forward from Seminary Ridge on July 3 toward the Union defensive line on Cemetery Ridge, defended by a good many Irishmen in blue, has also been overlooked historically.

James L. Kemper was a lawyer from Virginia who was wounded during "Pickett's Charge" and was captured by Federal forces.

On the afternoon of July 3, the largest Irish presence in "Pickett's Charge" was in the ranks of the First Virginia Infantry, Gen. James L. Kemper's Virginia brigade, Pickett's Division of Gen. James Longstreet's First Corps. The First Virginia had been organized by Col. Patrick Theodore Moore, Ireland-born from the seaport town of Galway in 1821. Moore immigrated to Richmond, Virginia, in 1844, and embarked upon a successful business career as a Richmond merchant. In 1850, Moore gained an added measure of status and prestige in Richmond society by becoming the captain of the Montgomery Guards, which he organized from among the many Irish citizens of Richmond. John Edward Dooley, a native of County Limerick in the picturesque Shannon River Country of the fertile midlands of Ireland, served as the first lieutenant of Captain Moore's Irish company during the ante-bellum period and in the First Virginia Infantry during the war years. Strengthening their ties to Irish nationalism, Captain

Moore and other Irishmen of the antebellum militia had become close associates to the exiled Irish revolutionary, John C. Mitchel, Sr., who made Richmond his home.

Green coats and kepis of the Irish soldiers of the Montgomery Guards proudly displayed the company's distinctive Celtic-Gaelic cultural heritage and ethnic composition. The Montgomery Guards was one of the mostly thoroughly Irish companies of the antebellum First Virginia regiment, though other Irishmen were sprinkled throughout the Old Dominion regiment. Not long after the Montgomery Guards departed Richmond for Harpers Ferry, Virginia, to put down John Brown's raid, Captain Moore became the colonel of the First Virginia and Lieutenant Dooley took command of the Montgomery Guards with a captain's rank.

With the opening of Confederate cannon on Fort Sumter, in the harbor of Charleston, South Carolina, in April 1861, hundreds of volunteers from Richmond's large Irish population of more than 2,200 flocked into the First Virginia's ranks. When the First Virginia Infantry engaged Federal troops in a new nation's struggle for self-determination, Ireland-born John Teeling served as the Catholic chaplain of the regiment, providing spiritual guidance to the Irish soldiers.

Immediately before the first major clash of the war in July 1861 near a muddy creek called Bull Run just west of Washington, D.C., the Irish Rebels of the First Virginia charged forward during the fighting at Blackburn's Ford with the Gaelic war-cry, "Faugh a ballagh," or "Clear the Way." This same battle-cry was employed by the soldiers of the Irish Brigade, Army of the Potomac—an illustration of just how deep cultural and ethnic heritage ran in the Irishmen on both sides.

In the First Virginia, the most symbolic Irish revolutionary presence could be found in the youngest son of Ireland's most famous revolutionary nationalist and political exile, John C. Mitchel, Sr., the former Protestant minister who was a leader of the Irish nationalists in the Young Ireland Movement of 1848. The movement sought separation from British rule. Like the son, the father often emphasized the analogy between the struggle for self-determination of the people of Ireland and the citizens of the Confederacy. William Henry "Willie" Mitchel, dark-haired and looking younger than his years, advanced forward with the lengthy line of First Virginia troops during "Pickett's Charge" as an esteemed member of the regimental color guard. In contrast to the older and more seasoned veterans of the First Virginia, "Willie" was anything but a grizzled, battle-hardened veteran. At age seventeen, "Willie" looked more like a school boy than any other member of the First Virginia's color guard, and he often acted his young age. The French-educated Mitchel was consumed with a boyish fascination with insects, and this penchant resulted in his nickname of "Bugalist" among the older troops. In fact, the holocaust of Gettysburg was William Mitchel's first battle after joining the First Virginia in November 1862. Despite his youth and inexperience, "Willie" Mitchel was entrusted with the prestigious duty of a color guard member. Such a coveted position was usually reserved for the most trust worthy and dependable veterans because the regimental battle-flag was a cherished emblem which was to be preserved at all costs. Hence, the guardians of the regimental banner were the elite. Clearly, the inspiring symbolism of the youngest son of one of Ireland's leading nationalists and revolutionaries was not lost to the First Virginia Irish.

As a cruel fate would have it, the teenage color guard's first time under fire was also William Mitchel's last. In the forefront of the First Virginia's ranks during "Pickett's Charge," "Willie" was hit and fell with a serious wound. Nevertheless, he refused to go to the rear along with the other wounded. Instead he continued to move forward with his Celtic compatriots to fulfill his role as a guardian of the regimental colors. He was struck again, and this time, the popular "Willie" was killed.

Upon learning of the tragic death of his youngest son, John Mitchel grieved as only a father could. Nevertheless, the stoic father responded to the grim news of his son's death by saying that "he could not have fallen in better company nor, as I think, in a better cause." For Mitchel, Sr. and so many other Confederate Irish, the struggle of self-determination of Ireland and the South were one and the same.

Capt. John C. Mitchel, Jr., was the son of Irish revolutionary John C. Mitchel, Sr. He served in the First South Carolina Artillery and was killed in the war. His two brothers, William and James, also served in the C.S.A.

But the Confederate Irish presence of the Mitchel family was not limited to "Willie." Mitchel's oldest son, Capt. John C. Mitchel, Jr., served with distinction in the First South Carolina Artillery. He later died in the defense of Fort Sumter in July 1864 while making observations in an exposed position during the siege. He "saw the shell coming, but refused to go to the bombproof as he felt he must set his men an example of courage." Revealing the extent of the influence that Ireland's revolutionary example yet existed in the hearts and minds of the Irish Confederate soldiery, the dying words of Captain Mitchell, only three hours after he had been wounded, were, "I die willingly for South Carolina, but oh! that it had been for Ireland!"

Yet another son of John C. Mitchel, Sr., served in the ranks of the First Virginia—Capt. James Mitchel. He commanded Company C, also known as the Montgomery Guards, which consisted of Irishmen from Richmond, Virginia. By the time of the battle of Gettysburg, Captain Mitchel was serving as a brigade staff officer. War became less of an abstract, idealistic struggle for the Mitchel family when James fell wounded during the vicious fighting at Second Manassas in late August 1862.

"Willie," James, and John, Jr., took much pride in the revolutionary role of their father. John C. Mitchel, Sr., was not only a primary leader of the Young Ireland Movement of 1848, but also a founder of the armed liberation movement of the late 1850s called the Fenian Brotherhood in the United States and the Irish Republican Brotherhood in Ireland. Based upon historic Irish nationalism, this pro-independence movement closely identified with the American patriots' struggle against the British during the American Revolution. Secret nationalist societies of Ireland named "Confederate Clubs" served as a foundation for the 1848 uprising. That uprising failed as well, and by the time of the Civil War, Irishmen who now found themselves in America related to the South's struggle for independence, much like their forefathers' earlier identification with the American colonists' struggle for independence. The American Revolution inspired the Irish uprising of 1798—the largest and most successful revolt in Irish history—and the failed revolt of Irish patriot Robert Emmet in 1803. In turn, both of these revolts inspired revolutionaries like John C. Mitchel, Sr., and the Young Ireland Movement in 1848. For the Civil War generation of Irishmen, the revolutionary tradition helped to sow the seeds for the widespread participation of Irish Rebels in the Civil War.

A long-standing tradition of fighting in defense of one's ancestral homeland and culture against a "foreign" adversary was a deeply-ingrained philosophical concept to the Confederate Irish of the First Virginia, especially John Mitchel's sons. Mitchel, Sr., thoroughly incorporated the revolutionary ideology and militant nationalism of the Young Ireland Movement in his 1850s writings as editor of the radical Dublin nationalist newspaper *The Nation*. Mitchel emphasized the importance of Irish nationalism, the historical past, the legacy of earlier struggles and rebellions against British authority, and the meaning of the concept of "dying for Ireland."

By 1861, a vibrant southern nationalism embraced these same themes. For the Mitchels and so many other Irish on both sides of the Atlantic, Irish "nationalism became a secular religion and a sacred faith, serving as the foundation for the Fenian spirit" of rebellion and revolution against British domination. Inspired by such potent revolutionary influences, the young Irish Confederates of the First Virginia marched forward to meet a cruel fate during "Pickett's

Charge" on the hot afternoon of July 3, 1863. They pushed toward Union-held Cemetery Ridge with not only pride in the centuries-long Irish revolutionary heritage and legacy of their Irish rebel forefathers but also in the rich Irish traditions of their regiment as well.

After the war, John Mitchel, Sr., was imprisoned with President Davis at Fortress Monroe, Virginia, on the shores of Chesapeake Bay. The epitaph on Mitchel's tomb in Charleston, South Carolina, epitomized the feelings of a good many Irish Confederates: "I could not fight for Ireland, so I chose to fight for the South."

CHAPTER 7

The Rebel Sons of Erin of the "Davis Guard" Rise to the Challenge at Sabine Pass

During the four years of conflict, no single performance of the Irish Confederates had a greater overall impact in a single contest than at the remarkable battle of Sabine Pass along the Texas coast of the Gulf of Mexico. Sabine Pass was located at the mouth of the Sabine River, which separated Texas from Louisiana. At this junction, a mere handful of Confederate Irish from the port cities of Galveston and Houston, Texas, rose to the challenge and overcame impossible odds. These Irish Confederates thwarted a powerful Federal invasion of Texas. The remarkable defense of Sabine Pass by twenty-five year-old Lt. Richard "Dick" Dowling and forty-six other Irishmen of the Davis Guards (Company F), First Texas Heavy Artillery, was described by Confederate President Davis as "without parallel in ancient or modern warfare."

The Davis Guards consisted of a high-spirited band of Irish laborers, some who worked on the docks of Galveston and some who worked construction on railroad gangs. With skilled ease, the burly Emerald Islanders efficiently manhandled two 24-pound smoothbores and four 32-pound smoothbores into position in the small, incomplete earthen structure called Fort Griffin. This solitary defensive position along

the broad waters of Sabine Pass was all that stood between Texas and President Lincoln's dream of the conquest of Texas. Hence, the stage was set for a dramatic showdown between a handful of Confederate Irish of the Davis Guards and the powerful Union invasion force numbering in the thousands.

Lt. Richard "Dick" Dowling was born near Tuam, in west Ireland in January 1837. In 1848, the brutal ravages of the Potato Famine forced "Dick" Dowling and his older sister Honora to leave Ireland for America. They started life anew in New Orleans, Louisiana,

Richard "Dick" Dowling was a successful businessman in Texas before and after the war.

and were joined by the rest of their family at a later date. For generations, the city of New Orleans, located just above the mouth of the Mississippi, served as the primary port of entry for the Irish who migrated to the Mississippi Valley.

During the antebellum period Dowling rose from an impoverished immigrant to a successful Houston businessman, though several personal tragedies dulled the glory of his accomplishments. While living in New Orleans with his family before moving farther west to Texas, Dowling lost both his parents, Mary and William Dowling, to a yellow fever epidemic that ravished New Orleans in the 1850s. The transplanted Irishman had to make his own way in life at an early age. He attended a Catholic school in Galveston and embraced the faith of his distant homeland with a passion. In October 1857 at the age of nineteen, Dowling opened up a successful saloon—both bar and billiards parlor—called "the Shades" in Houston, the first public facility in the growing city to have gas lamps. Even at this early age, Dowling demonstrated considerable financial and business skill, selling "the Shades" for a nice profit when a high price could be reaped from all of his hard work and sacrifice.

At the age of twenty-two, he purchased a larger and more lucrative business, another saloon called "the Bank of Bacchus." He provided the best quality liquor for his thirsty patrons. The house special was a drink called "Kiss Me Quick and Go." In addition, Dowling entered the world of finance. He offered high interest loans and check cashing for his customers at a place where funds were quickly spent buying refreshments. While reaping rewards as a businessman, financier, and saloon keeper, Dowling remained a devout Catholic, though his wife was Presbyterian. In November 1857, he had married a dark-haired beauty, Elizabeth Anne Odlum. Odlum came from one of the leading planter families of Houston area. In 1859, the same year as the birth of his first son, Dowling moved up another rung of the social ladder by joining a local militia unit, the Houston Light Artillery. In the ranks of the unit, Dowling learned the cannoneer's art under the command of his father-in-law. This knowledge would be fully utilized by him during the Civil War, and especially at Sabine Pass.

Harper's Weekly *interpretation of the Battle of Sabine Pass as it appeared in the October 10, 1863 issue.*

Despite his success and good fortune, Dowling was destined to suffer more tragedy in his personal life. His first son Benjamin died in 1862 at the age of three, and another son, William, perished in early 1864 not long after his first birthday. For the previously charmed "Dick" Dowling, the loss of his sons became the greatest tragedies of his life. The Union naval blockade of Galveston may have contributed to the deaths of his two sons, especially with the blockade denying the delivery of precious medicines.

Lieutenant Dowling and the Irishmen of the Davis Guards held firm at Fort Griffin on the west side of the Sabine River against the might of the Union flotilla on September 8, 1863. In a spirited defense the all-Irish garrison, despite enduring hours of steady bombardment, used their artillery with both speed and accuracy. The marksmanship of Pvt. Michael McKernan was especially effective against the vulnerable wooden hulls of the Federal warships. The fire of the Texas guns wreaked havoc among the Union troop transports. Dowling's Irishmen disabled two Union gunboats with well-placed shots as they entered the waters of Sabine Pass. When the battle was over, the Federal force lost almost 100 men, and 350 Union sailors were captured. No Irishmen within the walls of Fort Griffin were lost.

Under Dowling's inspired leadership and fighting to the Texas Revolution motto of "Victory or Death," this relative handful of Irish cannoneers successfully defended Sabine Pass against the odds. The Union invasion of Texas was thwarted. For the moment, Texas was saved from Federal invasion by these Irishmen in gray, who had accomplished the impossible with their determination to succeed at all costs: "Victory or Death!"

A complete list of the Irish Defenders of Sabine Pass

Patrick Abbott
Michael Carr
Abner R. Carter
Patrick Clair
James Corcoran
Hugh Deagan
Michael Delaney
Thomas Daugherty
John A. Drummond
Daniel Donovan
Richard W. Dowling
Michael Eagan
David Fitzgerald

James Fleming
John Flood
William Gleason
John Hassoff
James Higgins
Timothy Hurley
John Hennessey
Thomas Hagerty
Timothy Huggins
William Hardin
W.L. Jett
Patrick Malone
Thomas McKernon
John McKeever
Alexander McCabe
Timothy McDonough
Patrick McDonnell
John McGrath
John McNealis
Daniel McMurray
Michael Monoghan
Richard O'Hara
Laurence Plunkett
Edward Pritchard
Maurice Powers
Charles Rheins
Michael Sullivan
Patrick Sullivan
Thomas Sullivan
Matthew Walsh
Jack W. White
John Wesley
Joseph Wilson

Celtic-Gaelic Rebels of the Tenth Tennessee Infantry Regiment of Volunteers (Irish)

Certainly one of the most unique and colorful Irish units of the western Confederacy was the Tenth Tennessee Infantry Regiment of Volunteers (Irish). These Celts hailed from the ethnic enclaves in the middle Tennessee communities of Pulaski (Company H), Clarksville (Company I), and McEwen (Company A), though most came from the state capital of Nashville and comprised companies B, C, D, E, F, G, and K. The majority of these Irish soldiers were Catholics and Potato Famine Irish or the sons of parents who survived the famine, though they were led by mostly Irish Protestant officers.

Consisting primarily of common laborers, carpenters, and artisans, the Irish of Nashville during the 1850s formed a political and military body to consolidate power, enhance social standing, and to politically oppose the anti-Irish Know-Nothing Party. The enterprising immigrants established the appropriately named St. Patrick's Club in antebellum Nashville, and proudly dubbed themselves the "Sons of Erin." This fraternal organization served as the nucleus of an Irish militia unit that was organized in April 1861— the Tenth Tennessee Infantry Regiment of Volunteers (Irish). Randal W. McGavock became the group's commander, thanks in part to the support of the large, vibrant Irish community of Nashville.

The first military task for the former Irish laborers was to construct the key defensive positions on the Tennessee and Cumberland Rivers, Forts Henry and Donelson, respectively. In late May 1861 at Fort Donelson, the Tenth Tennessee Infantry Regiment of Volunteers (Irish) completed its organization, forming an ethnically distinct Irish Tennessee State militia regiment. These Irishmen in gray not only spoke a blend of middle Tennessee with an Irish brogue, but also Gaelic from the old country. On September 1, 1861, the Irishmen were transferred into Confederate service.

Early in the war, the Irish Tennesseans received a reputation for rowdiness and hard-drinking. Some soldiers were mere boys, such as fourteen-year-old Pvt. Daniel McCarthy of Company D. Older soldiers, such as the ever-popular Commissary Sgt. Bernard "Barney" McCabe and Capt. John G. "Gentleman Johnny" O'Neil, who led the Irish of Company A, held positions of more responsibility. Some Clarksville boys of Company D were laborers and blacksmiths from the Clarksville Iron Works. These Rebels marched to war under a colorful green battle-flag, decorated with the proud words "Sons of Erin" above the gold harp of Ireland, shamrocks, and the inspiring motto "Where Glory Waits You" below the Irish harp.

The Irish of the Tenth Tennessee demonstrated their typical Irish spunk when they brawled with the Irish of the First Kentucky Brigade (the Orphan Brigade), one of the elite combat units of the western Confederacy. The rowdy men battled each other as state and regimental pride and loyalty transcended ethnicity. This clash between Tennessee and Kentucky Irish in some ways indicated the extent of greater Americanization among southern Irish than Yankee Irish because they battled each other for state pride rather than ethnic pride.

The stubbornness of the Irish soldiers became evident when Confederate forces were bottled-up by the forces of Gen. Ulysses S. Grant in the sprawling earthen defensive bastion of Fort Donelson which overlooked the Cumberland River. After the fall of Fort Henry in early February 1862, Gen. Gideon Pillow ordered Company F to man an artillery position at the fort. The Irish Rebels refused to obey the order. Pillow had to personally convince these individualistic, clannish Irishmen to obey his orders, pleading his case before them with a sense of desperation, "I had Irishmen with me in the Mexican War, and at [the battle of] Belmont [Missouri], where they proved themselves equal to any of our soldiery." Only reluctantly and after Colonel McGavock's considerable urging did Company F's Irish Rebels finally decide among themselves that it would be best to obey the orders of the second highest ranking commander at Fort Donelson.

Gideon Pillow was a lawyer from Tennessee who is best remembered for his poor performance during the Battle of Fort Donelson.

When the Confederate Irishmen first heard the news of the imminent surrender of Fort Donelson to Grant, Colonel McGavock and his men planned a daring escape, refusing to submit to the surrender. They even contemplated swimming the rain-swollen Cumberland River. In the end, they surrendered with the garrison in a devastating Confederate defeat that opened up the Mississippi Valley and the vital southern heartland for more penetrating Union invasions in the future.

After the capture of Fort Donelson, Union troops transported the Tennessee Irish to northern prison camps. One of these notorious Union prisons was Camp Douglas, located outside Chicago, Illinois. Col. James A. Mulligan, the former leader of the "Irish Brigade of the West," was also at Camp Douglas. The young, handsome colonel and his men had been captured themselves while defending another fortified position at Lexington, Missouri, in September 1861 after a short siege by the Missouri Rebels under Gen. Sterling Price. Among "Old Pap" Price's forces—including many future members of the First Missouri Confederate Brigade—were Irish Confederates of the Missouri State Guard from St. Louis and rural counties, especially along the Missouri River.

After the survivors of Fort Donelson were exchanged and reenlisted into Confederate service, the Tenth Tennessee ceased to exist except in spirit, while McGavock's Tennessee Irish continued to fight on in what essentially became a

Harper's Weekly *picture of the Surrender of Fort Donelson as it appeared on the cover of the March 1, 1862 issue.*

sharpshooter detachment. The serviving Irish served faith-
fully in actions across the Western Theater.

Irishmen on both sides of the war continued to clash with
each other year after year. Tennessee Irish shot down Irish
members of the Union Seventh Missouri Volunteer Infantry
during the battle of Raymond, Mississippi, in the 1863
Vicksburg campaign. The former members of the Tenth
Tennessee fought on such bloody fields as Chickamauga,
Georgia, Nashville, and Bentonville, North Carolina, before
the war ended, along with their sacred dream of an independent Southern nation.

CONCLUSION

The important contribution of the Irish Confederates from 1861 to 1865 might well be described as one of the best untold stories of the Civil War. While the impressive role of the Irish who fought for the Union, especially in the Irish Brigade of the Army of the Potomac, has been popularized and even romanticized, the Irish Confederates have remained the Civil War's forgotten soldiers. Because the ill-fated Confederacy lost its bid for independence—like so many Irish revolts on the Emerald Isle itself over the span of hundreds of years—the sacrifices of the Irish Confederates have been lost to the pages of history, vanishing like the ambitious, grandiose dreams of an independent southern nation.

The overall importance of the Irish contribution to the Confederate war effort can be well understood by way of a simple, basic equation: while there were large numbers of Irishmen in the North, they did not flock to the colors like their brethren in the South. Southern Irishmen identified closely with the South's desire for independence, and an extraordinary proportion volunteered for Confederate service.

Throughout the war years, the Irish soldiers of the South earned an unmatched reputation as fierce fighters and diehard revolutionaries, continuing the traditions and lega-

cies of their homeland. The fact that Irish Confederate soldiers were widely acknowledged as the elite fighting men of
the South is in part revealed by an abundance of wartime letters, reports, diaries, and postwar reminiscences and memoirs of many non-Irish southern soldiers. Even though these
Protestant Southerners were anti-immigrant, anti-Catholic,
and anti-Irish in sentiment, they nevertheless often felt
obliged to repeatedly compliment the Irish for their courage.
Indeed, a direct correlation existed between the preponder-
ance of Irish soldiers in Confederate units—companies, regiments, and even brigades—that earned lofty reputations as
elite commands and the high casualty rates of those units.

The symbiotic relationship between elite combat qualities
of Confederate units and the extent of the unit's Irishness can
in part be explained by the fact that a clannish ethnic soli-
darity fueled and reinforced both esprit de corps and high
morale among the Irish soldiers. The Irish Confederates possessed visible and separate ethnic self-identities, a distinctive nationality, vibrant Celtic-Gaelic martial tradition, a
powerful sense of Irish pride, and unique cultural, historical
and revolutionary legacies that fused together during the war
years to create elite fighting men. High battlefield losses also
resulted from the determined efforts of the Irish Confederate
soldiers to fulfill the same sacred dream that had motivated
generations of Irishmen for hundreds of years on the Green
Isle: to win independence and freedom.

Since ancient times, historians from around the world
have explored the nature of warfare and contemplated upon
what factors were most responsible for creating choice warriors and crack military units. In the recent past, Civil War

historians have attempted to explain why some southern combat units outshone others so dramatically on the battlefield. Never before have the qualities of southern combat units and superior battlefield performances been explained in terms of their distinctive Celtic-Gaelic ethnic composition, cultural heritage, and the revolutionary traditions until the publication of this work.

The impressive roles played by the Irish Confederates from 1861–1865 can be neither fully appreciated nor understood without drawing upon the lessons and experiences derived from the troubled course of Irish history. In regard to the Irish Confederates, the turbulent Irish past and how the Irish people battled for centuries against a powerful centralized government in London and its invading armies provided a rich revolutionary historical tradition, and the enduring lessons of Irish history help to explain the course of not only Confederate history, but also American history, beginning with the American Revolution and including the Civil War.

Indeed, much can be explained by understanding the Irish experience not only in America, but also in Ireland. When examined in the terms of the dominance of Celtic-Gaelic culture, heritage, and traditions among southern people by the time of the Civil War, the distinguished performance and sacrafice of Irish Confederates in some of the best southern combat units on both sides of the Mississippi River becomes much more comprehensible.

BIBLIOGRAPHY

Alexander, Edward Porter. *Fighting for the Confederacy: The Personal Recollections of General Edward Porter Alexander.* (Chapel Hill: University of North Carolina Press, 1989).

Andrews, William H. *Footprints of a Regiment: A Recollection of the 1st Georgia Regulars, 1861-1865.* (Atlanta, Ga.: Longstreet Press, 1992).

Barton, George. *Angels of the Battlefield.* (Philadelphia: Catholic Art Publishers, 1897).

Bevier, Robert S. *History of the First and Second Missouri Confederate Brigades, 1861-1865.* (St. Louis: Bryan, Brand and Company, 1879).

Blackford, Charles M., III, ed. *Letters From Lee's Army.* (New York: Perpetua Books, 1962).

Boyce, Joseph. Missouri Historical Society Collection. St. Louis, Missouri.

Brooks, Thomas Walter and Michael Don Jones. *Lee's Foreign Legion: A History of the 10th Louisiana Legion.* (Gravenhurt, Ontario: Watts Printing, 1995).

Conyngham, David Power. *The Irish Brigade and Its Campaigns.* (New York: Fordham University Press, 1994).

Compiled Military Service Records of Confederate Soldiers who Served in Organizations from the States of Tennessee, Missouri, Virginia, Georgia, Kentucky, Louisiana, Mississippi, Texas, and Alabama; Library of Congress, Washington, D.C.

Conolly, Thomas. *An Irishman in Dixie: Thomas Conolly's Diary of the Fall of the Confederacy.* (Columbia, S.C.: University of South Carolina Press, 1988).

Daily Delta, New Orleans, La.

Davis, Graham. *Land! Irish Pioneers in Mexican and Revolutionary Texas.* (College Station: Texas A & M University Press, 2002).

Daily Dispatch, Richmond, Va.

"Defense of the Sabine Pass," Essays from the Irish Cultural Society of San Antonio, Texas.

Durkin, Rev. Joseph T. *John Dooley, Confederate Soldier: His War Journal.* (Washington, D.C.: Georgetown University Press, 1945).

Enquirer, Richmond, Va.

Fleming, Thomas. *Liberty: The American Revolution.* (New York: Penguin Group, 1997).

Foster, R.F., ed. *The Oxford History of Ireland.* (Oxford: Oxford University Press, 1992).

Foster, Samuel T. *One of Cleburne's Command: The Civil War Reminiscences and Diary of Capt. Samuel T. Foster, Granbury's Texas Brigade, C.S.A.* (Austin, Tex.: University of Texas Press, 1980).

Gannon, James P. *Irish Rebels: Confederate Tigers.*
(Campbell, Ca.: Savas Publishing Company, 1998).

Gleeson, David T. *The Irish in the South, 1815-1877.*
(Chapel Hill: University of North Carolina Press, 2001).

Gleeson, Ed. *Rebels Sons of Erin.* (Indianapolis, In.: Guild
Press of Indiana, 1993).

Jolly, Ellen Ryan. *Nuns of the Battlefield.* (Providence, R.I.:
Providence Visitors Center, 1927).

Jones, Terry. *Civil War Memoirs, Captain William J.
Seymour: Reminiscences of a Louisiana Tiger.* (Baton
Rouge: Louisiana State University Press, 1991).

Jones, Terry. *Lee's Tigers: The Louisiana Infantry in the
Army of Northern Virginia.* (Baton Rouge: Louisiana
State University Press, 1987).

Krick, Robert K. *Lee's Colonels: A Biographical Register of
the Field Officers of the Army of Northern Virginia.*
(Dayton, Oh.: Morningside Bookshop, 1992).

Lalor, Brian, ed. *The Encyclopedia of Ireland.* (New Haven,
Conn.: Yale University Press, 2003).

Lane, Mills, ed. *"Dear Mother: Don't Grieve about Me. If I
Get Killed, I'll Only Be Dead,": Letters of Georgia
Soldiers in the Civil War.* (Savannah, Ga.: Beehive Press,
1977).

Litton, Helen. *Irish Rebellions, 1798-1916.* (Dublin, Ireland:
Wolfhound Press, 1998).

Loehr, Charles T. *War History of the Old First Virginia
Infantry Regiment, Army of Northern Virginia.*
(Richmond, Va.: Ellis Jones, 1884).

Lonn, Ella. *Foreigners in the Confederacy*. (Chapel Hill: University of North Carolina Press, 2002).

Lucey, Charles. *Harp and Sword: 1776*. (Washington, D.C.: Colortone Press, 1976).

MacCall, Seamus. *Irish Mitchel: A Biography*. (London: Thomas Nelson, 1938).

McClendon, William A. *Recollections of War Times*. (Montgomery, Ala.: The Paragon Press, 1909).

McPherson, James M. *Battle Cry of Freedom: The Civil War Era*. (New York: Oxford University Press, 1988).

McWhiney, Grady. *Cracker Culture: Celtic Ways in the Old South*. (Tuscaloosa, Ala.: University of Alabama Press, 1988).

McWhiney, Grady, and Perry D. Jamieson. *Attack and Die: Civil War Military Tactics and the Southern Heritage*. (Tuscaloosa, Ala.: University of Alabama Press, 1982).

Memphis Daily Appeal, Memphis, Tenn.

Niehaus, Earl F. *The Irish in New Orleans, 1800-1860*. (Baton Rouge: Louisiana State University Press, 1965).

Oates, William C. *The War Between the Union and the Confederacy and Its Lost Opportunities with a History of the 15th Alabama Regiment and the Forty-Eight Battles in Which It was Engaged*. (Dayton, Oh.: Morningside Bookshop, 1985).

O'Brien, Kevin E. *My Life in the Irish Brigade: The Civil War Memoirs of William McCarter, 116th Pennsylvania Infantry*. (Campbell, Ca.: Savas Publishing Company, 1996).

Owen, William M. *In Camp and Battle with the Washington Artillery of New Orleans.* (Boston: Ticknor and Company, 1885).

Pender, William Dorsey. *The General To His Lady: The Civil War Letters of William Dorsey Pender to Fanny Pender.* (Chapel Hill: University of North Carolina Press, 1965).

Robertson, James I., Jr. *The Stonewall Brigade.* (Baton Rouge: Louisiana State University Press, 1963).

Sackett, Frances R. *Dick Dowling.* (Houston, Tex.: Gulf Publishing Company, 1937).

Stiles, Robert. *Four Years Under Marse Robert.* (Dayton, Oh.: Morningside Bookshop, 1977).

Sutton, E.H. *Civil War Stories.* (Demorest: Banner Printing Company, 1910).

Symonds, Craig L. *Stonewall of the West: Patrick Cleburne and the Civil War.* (Lawrence, Kan.: University Press of Kansas, 1997).

Tucker, Phillip Thomas. *Burnside's Bridge: The Climactic Struggle of the 2nd and 20th Georgia at Antietam Creek.* (Mechanicsburg, Penn.: Stackpole Books, 2000).

Tucker, Phillip Thomas. *Forgotten Stonewall of the West: General John Stevens Bowen.* (Macon, Ga.: Mercer University Press, 1996).

Tucker, Phillip Thomas. *Storming Little Round Top: The 15th Alabama and Their Fight for the High Ground, July 2, 1863.* (New York: Da Capo Press, 2002).

Tucker, Phillip Thomas. *The Confederacy's Fighting Chaplain: Father John B. Bannon.* (Tuscaloosa, Ala.: University of Alabama Press, 1992).

Tucker, Phillip Thomas. *The South's Finest: History of the First Missouri Confederate Brigade, From Pea Ridge to Vicksburg.* (Shippensburg, Md.: White Mane Publishing Company, 1993).

Tucker, Phillip Thomas. *Palmito Ranch: The Last Battle of the Civil War.* (Mechanicsburg, Penn.: Stackpole Books, 2001).

Tucker, Phillip Thomas. *Westerners in Gray: The Elite Fifth Missouri Confederate Infantry.* (Jefferson, N.C.: McFarland Press, 1995).

United States War Department, *The War of the Rebellion: A Compilation of the Official Records of the Union and Confederate Armies,* 130 vols. (Washington, D.C.: U.S. Government Printing Office, 1895-1919).

Wallace, Lee A. *1st Virginia Infantry.* (Lynchburg, Va.: H.E. Howard, 1984).

Warner, Erza J. *Generals in Gray.* (Baton Rouge: Louisiana State University Press, 1983).

INDEX